# 101 Ways
## To Make Your Students
## Better Decoders and Readers

## Contents

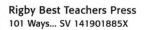

**Rigby Best Teachers Press**
101 Ways... SV 141901885X

# Introduction

Research indicates that two areas critical to reading development include phonemic awareness and phonics.

- **Phonemic Awareness** involves hearing and identifying the individual sounds, or phonemes, in words and how they can be manipulated to create new words.
- **Phonics** focuses on the written letters of the alphabet and their relationship to spoken sounds.

Before children can understand sound-symbol relationships (phonics), they must be able to hear and manipulate oral sound patterns (phonemic awareness). The Phonemic Awareness Interview on pages 3 through 9 will help you determine a child's level of phonemic awareness. To develop phonemic awareness, children must be exposed to rhymes, rhythms, songs, sounds, patterns, and the fun of oral language. Such activities can be found on pages 12 through 20.

In addition to phonemic awareness, phonics must be taught systematically and explicitly to ensure reading success. Activities that help children learn that there are relationships between written letters and spoken sounds can be found on pages 21 through 40.

*101 Ways to Help Your Students Become Better Decoders and Readers* also includes School-Home Newsletters and patterns for games and activities designed to help you put each child on the road to reading success!

Rigby Best Teachers Press
101 Ways... SV 141901885X

# Phonemic Awareness Interview

Phonemic awareness is an understanding that speech is composed of a series of sounds, or phonemes. Children who have difficulty attending to and manipulating the sounds in their language are likely to have problems learning to read. These children need additional experience with oral language play to heighten their sensitivity to the phonemic basis of their speech.

The Phonemic Awareness Interview is an oral test designed to provide informal assessment of a child's level of phonemic awareness to help the teacher plan for the development of literacy activities. The Phonemic Awareness Interview consists of the following four tasks:

**Task 1: Sound Matching**
Assesses the child's ability to tell whether the beginning sounds (phonemes) in words are the same or different

**Task 2: Sound Isolation**
Assesses the child's ability to produce the initial sound (phoneme) in words

**Task 3: Sound Blending**
Assesses the child's ability to blend isolated sounds (phonemes) together to form words

**Task 4: Sound Segmenting**
Assesses the child's ability to segment individual sounds (phonemes) in words

## General Directions for Administering

The Phonemic Awareness Interview should be conducted individually in a quiet and comfortable setting. By administering the Interview individually, the teacher can be sure the child is attending to the task and can gain insights into problems the child may be having.

You may use any one, or all, of the tasks. If you wish to obtain a comprehensive understanding of the child's phonemic awareness, administer all four tasks. If you are interested in evaluating a specific aspect of phonemic awareness, administer only those tasks that are relevant to your needs. Whether you administer all four tasks or just selected tasks, the tasks should be given in sequential order.

There is no time limit. However, a period of 15 to 20 minutes is suggested to administer all four tasks. If possible, the tasks should be administered in a single session.

You and the child should be seated at a flat table or desk. The best seating location for you is facing the child, to facilitate clear diction and immediate recording of responses.

Become familiar with the directions and items. Specific directions for administering each task can be found on each "Administering and Recording Form." The text in **bold** type is intended to be read aloud. The other information is for the teacher only and should not be read aloud. You should feel free to rephrase the directions, to repeat the samples, or to give additional examples to make sure the child understands what to do.

Before beginning the Interview, spend a few minutes in light, friendly conversation with the child. Don't refer to the Interview as a "test." Tell the child you would like to play some "word games."

## Specific Directions for Administering

Follow these steps to administer the Phonemic Awareness Interview:

1. Duplicate a copy of the "Administering and Recording Form" for each task you will be administering and one "Summary of Performance Form." You will record a child's responses on the "Administering and Recording Form" and summarize the totals on the "Summary of Performance Form." The child will not need any materials.

2. Explain that the words the child hears and says every day are made up of sounds and that you will be saying some words and sounds and asking questions about them. Be sure to speak clearly.

3. Administer the tasks in sequential order. If the child has difficulty with the first few items or cannot answer them, you may wish to discontinue conducting that particular task until a later time. If the child misses half of the items on any task, move on to the next task.

4. Follow the same basic procedures when administering each task. First, model the task so the child understands what to do. Second, administer the sample item and provide positive feedback to the child. Third, administer the items for that task. Fourth, record the child's responses for each item.

5. After the Interview, record the child's scores on the "Summary of Performance Form." Use the "Level of Performance" scale on the "Summary of Performance Form" to determine the level that best describes the child's understanding of phonemic awareness. Children whose scores reflect minimal or emerging understanding may need additional oral language experiences. You may also wish to record specific observations from the Interview, especially for those areas where the child had obvious difficulty with the task or required additional prompting.

# Phonemic Awareness Interview

## Summary of Performance Form

Name _____ Grade _____ Date _____

| Task | Score | Comments |
|------|-------|----------|
| Task 1: Sound Matching | _____ / 8 | _____ |
| Task 2: Sound Isolation | _____ / 8 | _____ |
| Task 3: Sound Blending | _____ / 8 | _____ |
| Task 4: Sound Segmenting | _____ / 8 | _____ |
| Total Phonemic Awareness | _____ /32 | _____ |

| Level of Performance (circle one): | | |
|---|---|---|
| Minimal | Emerging | Strong |
| 0–12 | 13–25 | 26–32 |

Comments:

# Phonemic Awareness Interview

## Task 1: Sound Matching Administering and Recording Form

Task:  The child will listen to two words and will indicate if the two words do or do not begin with the same sound.

Model:  **I am going to say two words. Listen carefully so you can tell me if the two words begin with the same sound:** *monkey, mother*. **Listen again:** *monkey, mother*. **The words begin with the same sound.** *Monkey* **and** *mother* **begin with the same sound.**

Sample:  **Listen to these two words:** *rain, snow*. **Listen again:** *rain, snow*. **Do the two words begin with the same sound?** (no) **You're correct.** *Rain* **and** *snow* **do not begin with the same sound.**

**Now listen to some more words. Tell me if the words begin with the same sound.**

Name _____ Grade _____ Date _____

|  | Circle child's response. (Correct response is underlined.) |  |
| --- | --- | --- |
| Items |  |  |
| 1. leg, lunch | <u>Same</u> | Different |
| 2. duck, pan | Same | <u>Different</u> |
| 3. sun, moon | Same | <u>Different</u> |
| 4. fork, fish | <u>Same</u> | Different |
| 5. chocolate, checkers | <u>Same</u> | Different |
| 6. phone, poem | Same | <u>Different</u> |
| 7. ball, banana | <u>Same</u> | Different |
| 8. red, nut | Same | <u>Different</u> |

Total Score: _____/8

Comments:

# Phonemic Awareness Interview

## Task 2: Sound Isolation Administering and Recording Form

Task: The child will listen to a word and then will produce the initial phoneme in the word.

Model: **I am going to say a word. Then I am going to say just the beginning sound. Listen carefully for the beginning sound:** *pig.* **The beginning sound is /p/.**

Sample: **Listen to another word. This time, you tell me the beginning sound. Listen carefully:** *goat.* **What is the beginning sound in** *goat*? (/g/) **You're correct. /g/ is the beginning sound in** *goat.* (*If the child tells you a letter name, remind the child to tell you the sound, not the letter.*)

**Now listen to some more words. Tell me the beginning sound you hear in each word.**

Name _____ Grade _____ Date _____

| Items | Correct Response | Child's Response |
|-------|------------------|------------------|
| 1. *d*ot | /d/ | _____ |
| 2. *m*ap | /m/ | _____ |
| 3. *s*ad | /s/ | _____ |
| 4. *t*alk | /t/ | _____ |
| 5. *c*ow | /k/ | _____ |
| 6. *b*ird | /b/ | _____ |
| 7. *f*arm | /f/ | _____ |
| 8. *y*ellow | /y/ | _____ |

Total Score: _____/8

Comments:

# Phonemic Awareness Interview

## Task 3: Sound Blending Administering and Recording Form

Task:       The child will listen to individual sounds and will blend the sounds together to say the word.

Model:      **I am going to say some sounds. Then I want you to put the sounds together to make a word. I will do the first one. Listen to the sounds: /r/-/u/-/n/. When I put the sounds /r/-/u/-/n/ together, they make the word *run*.**

Sample:     **Listen to these sounds: /k/-/a/-/t/. What word do you make when you put /k/-/a/-/t/ together?** (cat) **You're correct. The sounds /k/-/a/-/t/ make the word *cat*.**

**Now listen again. I will say some sounds. You put the sounds together to make a word and tell me the word.**

Name _____ Grade _____ Date _____

| Items | Correct Response | Child's Response |
|---|---|---|
| 1. /g/-/ō/ | go | _____ |
| 2. /sh/-/ē/-/p/ | sheep | _____ |
| 3. /j/-/u/-/m/-/p/ | jump | _____ |
| 4. /a/-/n/-/t/ | ant | _____ |
| 5. /h/-/o/-/t/ | hot | _____ |
| 6. /l/-/i/-/p/ | lip | _____ |
| 7. /d/-/e/-/s/-/k/ | desk | _____ |
| 8. /b/-/ī/ | by | _____ |

Total Score: _____/8

Comments:

Rigby Best Teachers Press
101 Ways... SV 141901885X

# Phonemic Awareness Interview

## Task 4: Sound Segmenting Administering and Recording Form

Task:        The child will listen to a word and then will produce each phoneme in the word separately.

Model:     **I am going to say a word. Then I am going to say each sound in the word. Listen carefully for each sound. The word is** *go*. **The sounds in** *go* **are /g/-/ō/.**
(*Be sure to articulate each sound separately. Do not simply stretch out the word.*)

Sample:    **Listen to this word. This time, you tell me the sounds in the word. Listen carefully:** *man*. **What sounds do you hear in** *man*? (/m/-/a/-/n/) **You're correct. The sounds in the word** *man* **are /m/-/a/-/n/.**

**Now listen to some more words. Tell me the sounds you hear in these words.**

Name _____ Grade _____ Date _____

| Items | Correct Response | Child's Response |
|-------|------------------|------------------|
| 1. dog | /d/-/ô/-/g/ | _____ |
| 2. keep | /k/-/ē/-/p/ | _____ |
| 3. no | /n/-/ō/ | _____ |
| 4. that | /th/-/a/-/t/ | _____ |
| 5. me | /m/-/ē/ | _____ |
| 6. do | /d/-/o͞o/ | _____ |
| 7. race | /r/-/ā/-/s/ | _____ |
| 8. in | /i/-/n/ | _____ |

Total Score: _____/8

Comments:

## Introduction

What is your main reason for teaching phonics? One of your goals may be to provide children with strategies they can use to help them learn to read and write. A strategy is not something children know, such as a rule; rather, it is something children do! Young children are limited in what they can read, so they need to develop the ability to figure out words. This introduction offers some strategies you can model and teach children to use so that they can become better decoders and readers.

### Keep these tips in mind when teaching phonemic awareness and phonics:

- Plan activities that will keep children actively engaged. Avoid activities that have the child sit passively.
- Plan activities that include variety so that children's different learning styles are considered. Activities might involve children with singing, rhythm, movement, drama, games, writing, drawing, and manipulating visual props.
- Keep the use of phonics jargon and rules at a minimum. Instead, model strategies that children can use when they read and write.
- Offer activities that have something for everyone. Begin an activity with a warm-up to review or reinforce, and end with a challenge. Offer one-on-one or small-group instruction for those who need extra support and more challenging interactive games and activities for those who can work on their own.
- Engage children in daily reading and writing activities so that they use what they learn.

### How can we help children hear sounds in words?

*Develop Phonemic Awareness*
The phonemically aware child knows that the spoken word *pig* has three sounds that can be segmented into /p/-/i/-/g/. This child can identify that the word begins with /p/ and ends with /g/. This child can also name other words that have the same beginning, middle, or ending sound as *pig*. Making children phonemically aware will help them recognize that speech is made up of a series of individual sounds. This awareness will lay the foundation for children to eventually be able to use phonics as a means to decode printed words. Activities that build phonemic awareness include rhymes, songs, riddles, and games that require the child to match sounds in words; blend sounds to form words; count phonemes in words; isolate or segment sounds in words; and delete, add, or substitute sounds to form new words.

### How can we help children see patterns in words?

*Word Building Strategy*
Give children letter cards to make words. Start with a vowel such as *a* or a phonogram such as *-at*. Use letter cards to form words such as *bat, rat, sat, mat, fat, cat, hat, chat,* and *flat*. A child who can use letters to form *at* and *cat* can be guided to read and spell other *-at* words.

*Word Sorting Strategies*
Word sorts help children discover spelling patterns. First, you can model the word sort, using familiar words. Group the words into categories, and then help children think of other words that fit the categories. These categories might include words that rhyme, begin with the same sound, end with the same sound, or share the same spelling for a given vowel sound. After guided practice,

# Better Decoders and Readers

children can sort their own sets of word cards independently or with partners. These sorts might later be written on a Word Wall or in columns in a notebook, or filed together in a word file. Following are some different kinds of word sorts:

> **Closed Sort** Teacher selects the categories and models the procedure.
>
> **Open Sort** Children sort words according to their own categories. They explain their choice of categories.
>
> **Blind Sort** In this variation of the closed sort, the teacher determines the categories. Then one child or the teacher can call out a word while another child points to the key word it would follow. Children are not using written words, so more attention is paid to sounds than visual patterns.
>
> **Writing Sort** In this variation of the closed and blind sort, the teacher calls out a word while the child writes it in the proper category.
>
> **Speed Sort** Once children are proficient at sorting, they can time themselves during each sorting activity and chart their progress.

*Word Wall Strategies*

The building of a Word Wall develops children's ability to see words in terms of letters and patterns that will help them become effective decoders. Word Walls provide opportunities for children to generate words and become an accessible resource for troublesome words and checking words in writing. Play guessing games with words on a wall, or have children make Wordo (a form of Bingo) games. Or, choose words from the wall to form different kinds of sentences for children to write each day. Some examples of different kinds of Word Walls follow:

> **Key Words on a Wall** As children are introduced to high-frequency words, add them to a Word Wall in alphabetical order. Draw a shape box around each word to emphasize its configuration, one strategy children use to recognize words.
>
> **Tricky Words on a Wall** Make a wall of words that are most often misspelled. List them alphabetically. Do at least one daily activity in which children find, write, and chant the spelling of some of these words. Use the words in context to check meaning.
>
> **Rhyming Words on a Wall** Words are listed in groups by spelling patterns, for example, words with the phonograms *-eet* and *-eat*. Play riddle games and write rhymes, using the list as a resource.
>
> **Portable Word Walls** Children can copy the words from the Word Wall onto file folders that can be carried to a desk, the library, or another classroom. As words are added to the Word Wall, do the same to the portable version.

# Phonemic Awareness

## Rhyming Activities

### Rhyme-a-Day

*Teacher Directed*

Start each day by teaching children a short rhyme. Periodically throughout the day, repeat the rhyme with them. Say the rhyme together, have them say it alone, pause and leave out words for them to insert, or ask volunteers to say each line. Children will develop a repertoire of favorite rhymes that can serve as a storehouse for creating their own rhymes.

### Rhyme in a Line

*Teacher Directed*

Have children form a line. Give the first child in line a picture card. Ask the child to say the picture name and a word that rhymes. The card is passed to the next child, who does the same. If some children need encouragement, provide a beginning sound for them. Once several words have been given, continue with a new picture card.

### Scavenger Hunt

*Independent*

Place around the classroom several picture cards of things that rhyme. Send a **small group** of children on a scavenger hunt to retrieve the pictures and then sort them into groups according to names that rhyme. You may also want to try an "open sort" by having children create categories of their own to sort the picture cards.

### Puppet Parade

*Teacher Directed*

Use the Finger Puppets patterns on page 63 to assess children's ability to recognize words that rhyme. Invite a **small group** to make puppets by drawing certain objects or animals whose names rhyme with words you will say. For example, children in a group of four can decide who will make a finger puppet of a cat, a dog, a pig, and a cow. Then say words such as *frog, wig, sat, now, jig, bat, bow, hog, hat, how, log,* and *big*. The child who is holding the puppet whose name rhymes should wiggle it.

Rigby Best Teachers Press
101 Ways... SV 141901885X

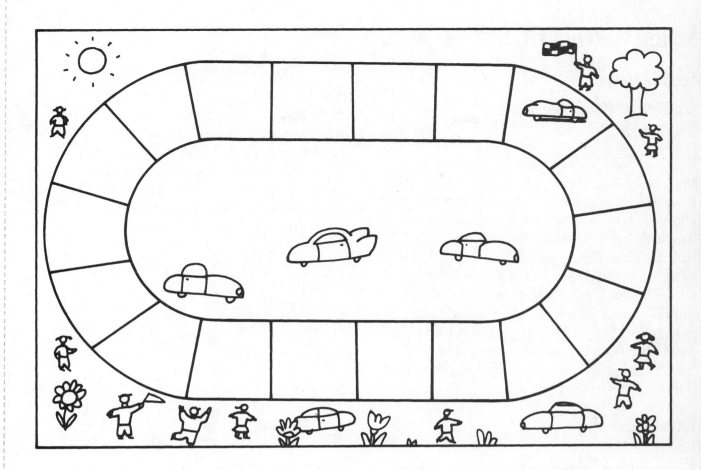

## Rhyme Pairs

*Teacher Directed*

To assess children's ability to recognize pairs of words that rhyme, say a list of twenty or more pairs of words. Half of the word pairs should rhyme. Children tell which word pairs rhyme and which do not. If working with a **small group,** have children indicate *yes* with a smiling face card or other symbol. If working with **one child** (or a small group), help children make a Racetrack Game Board using the pattern from page 53. For each correct response, the player can move a marker ahead one space. Provide word pairs until the player has finished the race.

## What Word Rhymes?

*Teacher Directed*

Use theme-related words from across the curriculum to focus on words that rhyme. For example, if you are studying animals, ask: *What rhymes with snake? bear? fox? deer? ant? frog? goat? hen? fish? whale?* If a special holiday is approaching, ask: *What rhymes with trick? treat? mask? scare? night?* Use these word groups for sound matching, sound blending, or sound segmenting activities.

# Sound Matching Activities

## Sound Seats

*Teacher Directed*

Arrange chairs in a circle with the backs facing inward. Include a chair for each child. Explain that you want children to listen for words that begin with the same sound as in *march*. Direct children to march around the chairs as you slowly say a list of words, some of which begin with the sound of *m*. Each time children hear a word that begins like *march*, they are to sit in the nearest chair. Say words such as *march, sing, moon, ball, cat, monkey, man, top, nest, mouse, seal, mop, fish, zebra, fan, milk,* and *map*. Continue the game, focusing on a different action and a new initial sound, such as flapping their arms if a word begins like *fly*.

## Picture Slide Show

*Independent*

Have children work in **pairs** or independently to draw pictures or search through magazines for pictures whose names begin with a given sound. The pictures can be cut out and glued on the slide from any Word Slide pattern on pages 64–68. Tape additional strips together to make a longer slide. Once the slides have been put together, suggest that children exchange slides with one another, naming each picture as the slide is pulled. Then children can work together to make up alliterative sentences and stories about the pictures.

## Odd Word Out

*Teacher Directed*

Form a **group** of four children. Say a different word for each group member to repeat. The child with the word that does not begin (or end) like the other words must step out of the group. For example, say *ball, bat, cow, box*. The child whose word is *cow* steps from the group. The odd-word-out player then chooses three children to form a new group and the procedure continues.

## Head or Toes, Finger or Nose?

*Teacher Directed*

Teach children the following rhyme. Be sure to say the sound, not the letter, at the beginning of each line. Recite the rhyme together several times while touching the body parts.

> */h/ is for head.*
> */t/ is for toes.*
> */f/ is for finger.*
> */n/ is for nose.*

Explain that you will say a list of words. Children are to touch the head when you say a word that begins with /h/, the toes for words that begin with /t/, a finger for words that begin with /f/, and the nose for words that begin with /n/. Say words such as *fan, ten, horn, hat, feet, nut, ham, nest, toy, fish, note, tub, nail, time, fox,* and *house*.

## Say and Sort

*Independent*

Have children work in **small groups.** Give each group a set of picture cards whose names begin with two or three different beginning consonant sounds. Group members are to say the picture names and sort the cards according to beginning sounds. The same activity can be used for sorting picture cards into groups whose names have the same medial or ending sound. As an alternative, allow children to create their own categories to sort a group of picture cards. A group of objects, such as toys, can be used in place of picture cards.

## Souvenir Sound-Off

*Teacher Directed*

Have children imagine that a friend has traveled to a special place and has brought them a gift. Recite the following verse, and ask a volunteer to complete it. The names of the traveler, the place, and the gift begin with the same letter and sound.

| | |
|---|---|
| My friend [person] who went to [place] brought me back a [gift]. | My friend Hannah who went to Hawaii brought me back a hula skirt. |

After repeating this activity a few times, ask **partners** to recite the verse to each other, filling in the missing words. With older children, you can focus on words with initial blends and digraphs. Children can focus on social studies and phonics skills by using a world map or globe to find names of places.

## Match My Word

*Teacher Directed*

Have children match beginning or ending sounds in words. Seat children on the floor in a circle, with **pairs** sitting back-to-back. One child in each pair will say a word. His or her partner will repeat the word and say another word that begins with the same sound. To invite each child to give a word, the group sings the following song to the tune of "The Farmer in the Dell."

(Child's name) will say a word.
Then you say the word.
Think of another word to say
That starts (ends) in the same way.

Begin with one child and move around the circle clockwise until each pair of children has had a turn to give a word and match a sound. Then repeat the activity, reversing the roles of partners and focusing on ending sounds.

## Coin Toss

*Independent*

Have children make a game board using the pattern for the 16-square grid on page 62. They should use rubber stamps or stickers to fill each space with a picture. **Partners** toss a coin or button on the grid, name the picture landed on, and say another word that begins (or ends) with the same sound.

# Sound Isolation Activities

## What's Your N-N-N-Name?

*Teacher Directed*

Invite children to say their names by repeating the initial phoneme in the name, such as *M-M-M-Michael* or by drawing out and exaggerating the initial sound such as *Sssssss-erena*.

## R-r-r-repeat the S-s-s-sounds

*Teacher Directed*

Sing a song that makes use of alliteration in the beginning sounds of words. "Hippity Hop to Bed" is an example that repeats the /h/ sound throughout. As you recite or sing the song, emphasize the /h/ sound by repeating it each time it occurs in the initial position.

H-h-h-hippity h-h-h-hop to bed,
I'd rather stay up instead.
But! When Daddy says "must,"
there's nothing else, just
H-h-h-hippity, h-h-h-hoppity;
H-h-h-hippity, h-h-h-hoppity,
H-h-h-hippity, h-h-h-hoppity;
H-h-h-hippity, h-h-h-hoppity, h-h-h-hop!
To bed!

## Sound-Off

*Teacher Directed*

Model how phonemes can be isolated in a word: *jam* starts with /j/; *goat* ends with /t/; and *cat* has the /a/ sound in the middle. Form **groups of three** children. Have them form a line, and designate which child will listen for the beginning, the middle, and the ending sound in words you say. Say a word and point to a child, who will then isolate and say the sound he or she is responsible for.

## Singling Out the Sounds

*Independent*

Form **groups of three** children. Children can decide who will name the beginning, the middle, and the ending sounds in one-syllable picture names. Given a set of picture cards, the group identifies a picture name, and then each group member isolates and says the sound he or she is responsible for. Group members can check one another.

## Chain Reaction

*Teacher Directed*

Have children form a circle. The child who begins will say a word such as *bus*. The next child must isolate the ending sound in the word, /s/, and say a word that begins with that sound, such as *sun*. If the word is correct, the two children link arms, and the procedure continues with the next child isolating the final sound in *sun* and giving a word that begins with /n/. You will want all children to be able to link arms and complete the chain, so provide help when needed.

# Sound Addition, Deletion, or Substitution Activities

## Add-a-Sound

Explain that the beginning sound is missing in each of the words you will say. Children must add the missing sound and say the new word. Some examples follow.

### Add:

| | | |
|---|---|---|
| /b/ to *at (bat)* | /f/ to *ox (fox)* | /k/ to *art (cart)* |
| /f/ to *ace (face)* | /p/ to *age (page)* | /h/ to *air (hair)* |
| /w/ to *all (wall)* | /j/ to *am (jam)* | /r/ to *an (ran)* |
| /b/ to *and (band)* | /d/ to *ark (dark)* | /f/ to *arm (farm)* |
| /d/ to *ash (dash)* | /s/ to *it (sit)* | /s/ to *oak (soak)* |
| /h/ to *eel (heel)* | /b/ to *end (bend)* | /m/ to *ice (mice)* |
| /n/ to *ear (near)* | /f/ to *east (feast)* | /b/ to *each (beach)* |
| /fl/ to *at (flat)* | /sk/ to *ate (skate)* | /tr/ to *eat (treat)* |
| /gr/ to *ill (grill)* | /sh/ to *out (shout)* | /pl/ to *ant (plant)* |

## Remove-a-Sound

Reinforce rhyme while focusing on the deletion of initial sounds in words to form new words. Ask children to say: *hat* without the /h/ *(at)*; *fin* without the /f/ *(in)*; *tall* without the /t/ *(all)*; *box* without the /b/ *(ox)*; *will* without the /w/ *(ill)*; *peach* without the /p/ *(each)*; *nice* without the /n/ *(ice)*; *meat* without the /m/ *(eat)*; *band* without the /b/ *(and)*. Continue with other words in the same manner.

$$box - /b/ = ox$$

## Rhyming Riddles

Play a word riddle game to focus attention on initial sounds in words and to reinforce rhyme and sound substitution. Ask children rhymes such as these:

- What color name rhymes with **bed** and begins with /r/? *(red)*
- What animal name rhymes with **hat** and begins with /k/? *(cat)*
- What food name rhymes with **Sam** and begins with /h/? *(ham)*
- What body part rhymes with **go** and begins with /t/? *(toe)*
- What furniture name rhymes with **fed** and begins with /b/? *(bed)*
- What number word rhymes with **hive** and begins with /f/? *(five)*

Continue the game with riddles of your own. Encourage children to create riddles, too.

## Sounds in Songs

*Teacher Directed*

Substitute sounds in words that occur in songs familiar to children. Choose songs that have adaptable refrains or make use of nonsense words.

"Old MacDonald Had a Farm"
    Ee-i, ee-i, oh
    Tee-ti, tee-ti, toh!
    Me-my, me-my, moh!

"Looby Loo"
    Here we go looby loo;
    here we go looby light...
    Here we go dooby doo;
    here we go dooby dight...
    Here we go gooby goo;
    here we go gooby gight...

Just for fun, when a child's birthday occurs, sing the words to the birthday song, substituting each beginning phoneme with that in the child's name:

    Mappy Mirthday mo mou!
    Mappy Mirthday mo mou!
    Mappy Mirthday mear Margie.
    Mappy Mirthday mo mou!

## Mixed-Up Tongue Twisters

*Teacher Directed*

Think of a simple tongue twister such as *ten tired toads*. Say the tongue twister for children, but replace the initial letter in each word with another letter, such as *p,* to create nonsense words: *pen pired poads*. Explain to children that you need their help to make sense of the tongue twister by having them replace /p/ with /t/ and say the new tongue twister. Use the same procedure for other tongue twisters. Then ask **partners** to do this activity together.

## The Name Game

*Independent*

Occasionally when a new sound is introduced, children might enjoy substituting the first sound in their names with the featured sound for the day. Children will have to stop and think when they call one another by name, including the teacher. For example, if it is /p/ day, *Ms. Vega* becomes *Ms. Pega,* *Carmen* becomes *Parmen,* *Jason* becomes *Pason,* and *Kiyo* becomes *Piyo.* Just make certain beforehand that all the names will be agreeable.

To make certain that children remember the sound of the day, have each child make a finger puppet with a picture whose name begins with the sound. Use the Finger Puppets patterns from page 63. For example, on /p/ day, everyone can make a pig finger puppet. The puppet can then go home with children to share with family members.

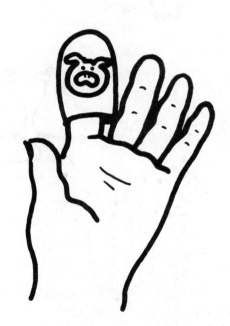

# Sound Blending Activities

## Do You Know Your Name?

*Teacher Directed*

Occasionally when it's time for children to line up for lunch, for dismissal, or to travel to another room, call their individual names aloud by segmenting the sounds. The child then blends the sounds to say his or her name and gets into line.

**/j/ - /e/ - /n/ -/i/ - /f/ - /ər/
Jennifer!**

As an alternative, you could provide an initial sound, and invite children whose names begin with that sound to line up.

## Listen to the Sounds

*Teacher Directed*

Sing the following song to the tune "Frère Jacques" to focus on blending sounds to form a word.

> **Make these three sounds;
> Make these three sounds:**
> **/k/-/a/-/t/.** (Children repeat:
>   /k/-/a/-/t/.)
> **Can you say the word?**
> **Can you say the word for**
> **/k/-/a/-/t/?** (Children repeat:
>   /k/-/a/-/t/.)

After a volunteer responds, repeat the song, inserting new sounds for words.

## Show Me the Picture

*Teacher Directed*   *Independent*

Display a set of picture cards or big alphabet cards. Make certain children know the name of each picture. Model how to say the name of one picture by segmenting the sounds, and ask children to identify it: *Show me the picture of the /f/-/r/-/o/-/g/.* As the picture is identified, have the **group** say its name by blending the sounds *(frog)*. Continue until

all the pictures have been identified. Provide new picture cards for children to continue this activity in **small groups**.

## I Bought Me a Cat

*Teacher Directed*

Display picture cards of animals, including one of a cat. Recite or chant the following Mother Goose rhyme:

> **I bought me a cat and the
>     cat  pleased me.**
> **I fed my cat by yonder tree;**
> **Cat goes fiddle-i-fee.**

Ask a volunteer to find and hold the picture of the cat. Then explain that you will say a new verse, but that you will say the next animal name in a special way. Ask children to figure out the name by blending the sounds together:

> **I bought me a /d/-/u/-/k/...**

Pause for children to blend the sounds to say *duck*. Then a volunteer can find the picture of the duck to hold. Recite the verse together, asking the child with the picture to suggest the sound the duck makes. Repeat the verse, inserting a new animal name each time.

# Sound Segmenting Activities

## How Many Sounds?

Teacher Directed

Provide children with concrete representations of sounds in words by having them use buttons or plastic counters. Each counter they show will represent one sound in a given word. For example, say the word *cat* and have the child repeat it. The child would represent the sounds in the word with three counters, and the word *flat* by four. The counters will gradually give way to letter cards.

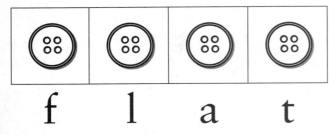

## Sound Counters

Independent

Provide **partners** with big alphabet cards and a set of counters. Children say each picture name together, decide how many sounds they hear in the name, and indicate the number of sounds by placing the same number of counters on the picture card.

## Pull the Word Apart

Teacher Directed

Provide **each child** with plastic tokens or buttons. Children will use these tokens to represent individual sounds in words. Recite this rhyme:

> Listen to my word.
> Tell me all the sounds you heard.
> [Say a word such as *stop*.]

Children will then separate and say each spoken sound in the word, /s/-/t/-/o/-/p/, and indicate the number by showing four tokens.

## Sound Game

Independent

Have **partners** play a word-guessing game, using a variety of picture cards or big alphabet cards that represent different beginning sounds. One child says the name of the card, separating the beginning sound, as in **d-og**. The partner blends the sounds and guesses the word. After children are proficient with beginning sounds, you could have them segment all the sounds in a word when they give their clues, as in **d-o-g**.

Rigby Best Teachers Press
101 Ways... SV 141901885X

## Activities for Consonants

You can duplicate and send home School-Home Newsletter 1, page 42, to provide families with fun, easy-to-do activities for reinforcing consonants.

### Jump-Rope Jingles

*Teacher Directed*

Children can start with their own names to review initial consonants in words. Write each line of the following jump-rope jingle on separate strips of tagboard, and place them in a pocket chart.

____my name is_____.

My friend's name is_____.

We come from_____.

And we like _____.

Model how children are to complete the rhyme, using the initial letter in your name.

> *K my name is Kathy.*
> *My friend's name is Kevin.*
> *We come from Kansas,*
> *And we like kangaroos.*

Provide blank cards for children to write the initial letter in their names and words that begin the same to complete the rhyme. Take turns inserting the cards into the pocket chart and chanting one another's rhymes. Use with a jump-rope to chant during recess.

Children may also enjoy making a pop-up book of their rhyme with the final word written and drawn inside the book on the part that can be popped up. Use the Pop-Up Book pattern from page 71.

Kangaroos

### Alphabet Puppet

*Teacher Directed*

Provide copies of the Finger Puppets patterns on page 63. Have each member of a **small group** make two letter puppets. Tell them the consonants they should write. As you say words, the child holding the puppet with the letter that stands for the beginning sound should wiggle it. Follow a similar procedure to reinforce ending consonant sounds in words, as well as consonant clusters and digraphs.

## Consonant Tic-Tac-Toe

*Independent*

Make copies of the 9-Square Grid on page 61. Make sure children know how to play the game Tic-Tac-Toe. Invite **pairs** of children to play, but in place of using X's and O's, assign a consonant to each player. Players can write the consonant on each of the game playing cards (five each). To make a move, the player must say 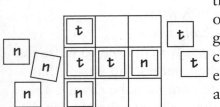 a word that begins with the letter sound and then place the letter card on the board. For each new game, children can change partners and trade letter cards. Older children can use the game to reinforce words with consonant clusters, digraphs, and *r*-controlled vowels.

## Happy Birthday to Me!

*Independent*

Provide patterns for the Step-Page Book from page 72. Once the books are assembled, invite children to wish themselves a *Happy Birthday* by giving themselves presents whose names begin with the sounds of four letters given by you. As  you name each of the four letters, children can write one on the bottom of each of the four pages. Then they can draw pictures or cut pictures from magazines of four gifts they would like. Later, have them finish writing the name of each present.

## Beginning or Ending Sound?

*Teacher Directed*

Provide **each child** with a plastic marker or button and a grid with three boxes. Say words that contain three phonemes and begin or end with the sound of a consonant you wish to reinforce. For example: *Where do you hear the /d/ sound in* red?

The child can indicate where the sound occurs in the word by placing the token on the corresponding box. To verify, have a volunteer form the word using *Letter Cards*.

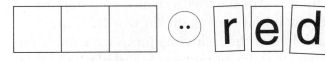

## Beginning and Ending Match

*Independent*

Use a picture sort to match initial and final consonant sounds in word pairs; for example, the beginning sound in *red* matches the end sound in *bear*. Provide the picture cards. Make certain that children can recognize the pictures and identify the beginning and ending sounds in each picture name. Model saying words that make a match. Then have **partners or a small group** work independently to sort sets of pictures. Provide an answer sheet with word pairs for checking. Here are two sample sets to get you started:

**Set One:**

| | | | |
|---|---|---|---|
| *bug / tub* | *rain / door* | *goat / rug* | *king / rock* |
| *lock / hill* | *nest / pin* | *pig / mop* | *tape / tent* |

**Set Two:**

| | | | |
|---|---|---|---|
| *pan / cup* | *rose / pear* | *seal / lips* | *tent / hat* |
| *girl / dog* | *lake / doll* | *nail / sun* | *duck / road* |

## Test Your Memory

### Teacher Directed

Display a group of objects. Choose objects with simple names. Have children identify the objects whose names begin with the same sound and remove the others. Then choose one of the following activities to do:

- Have children close their eyes as you remove one object. After they open their eyes, they can write the name of the missing object on paper. Reveal the object, and ask a volunteer to write the name on the board and underline the letter(s) that stand for the beginning sound(s).

- Cover the objects, and challenge children to write the names of as many objects as they can remember. As volunteers write each name on the board, show the object again. Have the volunteer underline the letter(s) that stand for the beginning sound(s).

Use more difficult words with older children to reinforce initial consonant clusters, digraphs, or names with like vowel sounds, including vowel variants.

## Begin-and-End-the-Same Game

### Independent

Make copies of the Racetrack Game Board on page 53, and assemble the track. In each section, write an easy word that begins and ends with a consonant. **Two or three players** can use game markers and a numbered spinner, found on page 60, to move along the game board. Players must read the word landed on and then say a word that begins with the same letter and sound. Next they say a word that ends with the same letter and sound. Play until everyone has circled the track.

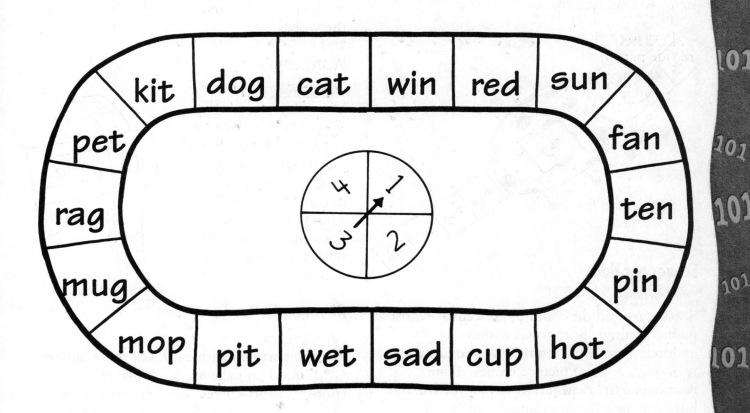

# Activities for Short Vowels

 You can duplicate and send home School-Home Newsletter 2, page 43, to provide families with fun, easy-to-do activities for reinforcing short vowels.

## Animal Word Slides

*Independent*

Patterns are provided on pages 64–68 to make animal Word Slides featuring words containing each of the short vowel sounds. Children can cut out the animal and the strip. Working **independently or with a partner,** they can name the animal and other people, places, and things with the same vowel sound and write the names in the sections on the strip. Make the strip longer by taping additional sections of paper together so more words can be added. Then have children insert the strip through the slits and pull through to read the words. Children can trade strips to read one another's words.

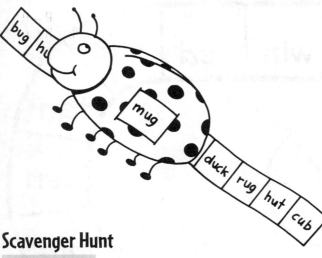

## Scavenger Hunt

*Independent*

Scatter around the room picture cards whose names contain short vowel sounds. Have children form **small teams,** and provide each team with a list of picture names. Team members must read the words on the list and hunt for the corresponding picture cards. When the hunt has ended, ask each group to match their words with the pictures they found to verify. This same activity can be used for words with long vowel sounds or initial consonant clusters. If you wish to make this a rhyming word activity, scatter word cards around the room, and provide a list of words that rhyme to match.

## Word Puzzlers

*Independent*

On the board, make several word puzzle boxes, with three boxes across and three down. Fill the first two boxes in the row going across with a consonant and vowel. **Pairs** of children can add letters to the puzzle to form two words. Repeat the activity, providing only the vowel in the middle box. Then have children start their own puzzle boxes for one another. Older children can create puzzles with more boxes for longer words and ask each other to write the words.

## Wordscopes

*Independent*

Have children use the Wordscope pattern on page 70. A phonogram can be written in the box on the scope, and letters that stand for beginning sounds are written on the strip, which is then pulled through the scope and read.

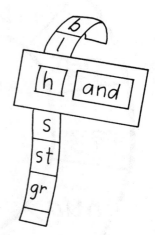

## Rhyming Tic-Tac-Toe

*Independent*

Provide **partners** with copies of the 9-Square Grid found on page 61. Each player must choose a short vowel phonogram to use in place of X's and O's. Players can write their chosen phonogram on each of the game playing cards (five each). To make a move, a player must say a word that ends with the chosen phonogram, spell the word aloud, and then place the phonogram card on the board. For each new game, children can change partners and trade phonogram cards.

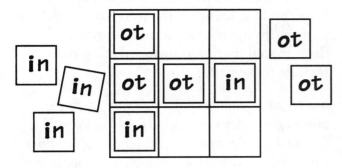

## Flip-the-Flap Books

Use the Flip Book pattern found on page 73 to have **individuals** make flip books that feature a short vowel phonogram, such as *ot*. Model by writing the letters *ot* on the larger strip. Write consonants, clusters, and digraphs on the smaller strips ( *n, c, g, h, d, l, p, r, bl, sl, tr, sh*). Show children how to assemble the book by stapling the stack of smaller strips onto the left side of the longer strip.

Plan which phonogram each child will do or have children decide. Then they can create a collection of different books for everyone's use. Suggest that children share their book pages with several partners before stapling them. **Partners** might suggest additional letters that can be added to form words.

## Trail Blazers

Make copies of the S-Shape Game Board on pages 55–56. In each section on the game board trail, write the beginning and ending letters to form a short vowel word. Insert a blank to indicate the missing vowel. Provide a numbered spinner, found on page 60, and game markers for each **group** of players. The object is to have players make as many words as possible.

1. First player spins and moves the number of spaces indicated.
2. All players look at the unfinished word and write a word on paper by inserting a vowel. Each player reads the word on his or her list. Players should brainstorm to determine if any other words can be made and written. The game continues with the next player spinning.
3. Play until everyone has reached the end of the trail.

These word frames could be used in the spaces on the board:

h_t  f_n  p_g  b_g  c_t  p_n
d_g  s_d  l_ck  r_g  r_ck  h_m
b_d  c_p  l_d  m_t  n_t  p_t
r_d  s_n  t_p  t_ck

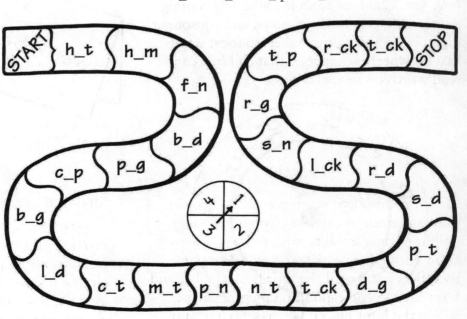

# Activities for Long Vowels

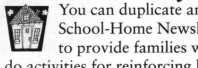

You can duplicate and send home School-Home Newsletter 3, page 44, to provide families with fun, easy-to-do activities for reinforcing long vowels.

## Making Words with Long Vowels

*Teacher Directed*

Follow the directions from previous activities to make flip books and wordscopes. Focus on long vowel spelling patterns.

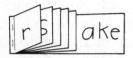

## Long-Vowel Word Wheels

*Independent*

Duplicate the Word Wheel pattern on page 69. Have children cut out and assemble the wheel with a paper fastener. Have **each child** write letters that spell a long vowel pattern on the left side of the top wheel. Suggestions: *ade, ail, ain, ake, ame, ate, ave, ay, eak, eam, eed, eel, eep, ice, ide, ight, ike, ind, ine, ite, oke, old, ole, one, ope.* Children finish the wheel by writing consonants, consonant clusters, and consonant digraphs on the bottom wheel to form words. Have a wheel exchange so that children can read words on several wheels.

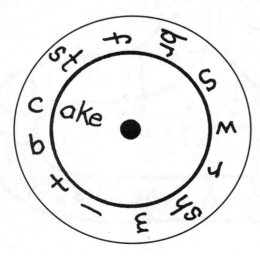

## Picture These Rhyming Pairs

*Teacher Directed*     *Independent*

Write the following words on index cards, or use the Word Cards pattern from page 75. To help children focus on the long vowel spelling pattern/rhyme relationship in words, have them match words to form rhyming pairs. Include these pairs:

| | | | |
|---|---|---|---|
| *beast feast* | *pink drink* | *brain strain* | *fly pie* |
| *bright light* | *clay tray* | *cold gold* | *dry fly* |
| *fake snake* | *fine pine* | *free bee* | *nice price* |
| *pale whale* | *rock clock* | *snail jail* | *weak beak* |

Invite **each child** to choose a word pair to illustrate in a funny manner. Children can also create rhyming word pairs of their own and illustrate them. Note that the long vowel spelling does not always have to be the same—for example, *sweet treat* and *cheap sheep*. This same activity can be used with short vowel words. These illustrations can be published using the Pop-Up Book pattern on page 71. Children can write the rhyming word pair on the front and have their picture pop up from inside.

Rigby Best Teachers Press
101 Ways... SV 141901885X

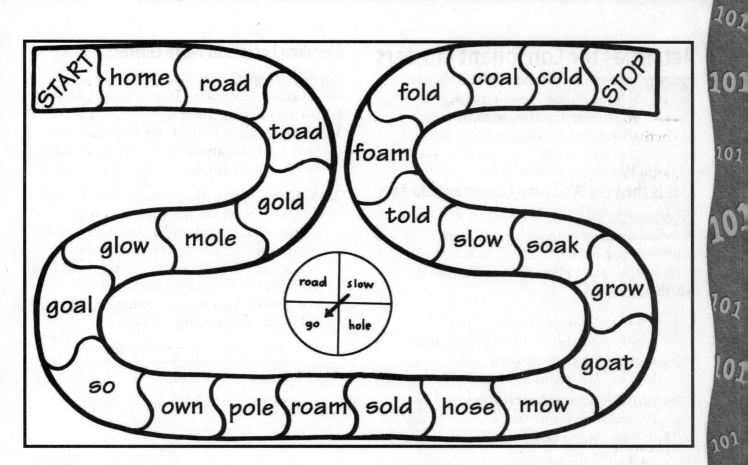

## Go Slow on the Road

**Independent**

Make a copy of the S-Shape Game Board
from pages 55–56. Fill the spaces with words
containing the long *o* vowel sound, spelled *oa,
o-e, ow,* and *o.* Use the blank spinner pattern
from page 60, and draw lines to divide the
spinner into four sections. Write one of the
following words in each section: *road, slow, go,
hole.* **Two or three players** take turns spinning,
reading the word on the spinner, moving a game
marker along the road to the first word that
contains the same spelling for the vowel sound
of long *o,* and reading the word.

## Guess My Picture Name

**Independent**

Provide **each child** with a copy of the Pull-Out
Book pattern on page 74. Model how children
are to write a list of words with long vowel
sounds on the page. Then they are to choose
one of those words to illustrate on the pull-
out tab. After their books are assembled, they
can tell a **partner** clues, and ask him or her to
read the list and guess which word is pictured
on the hidden tab.

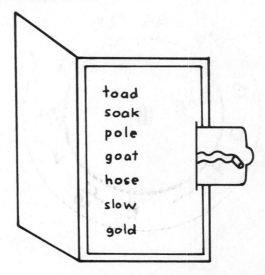

# Activities for Consonant Clusters

You can duplicate and send home School-Home Newsletter 4, page 45, to provide families with fun, easy-to-do activities for reinforcing consonant clusters.

## This Is the Way We Learn Consonant Clusters

*Teacher Directed*

Provide children with individual Letter Cards, found on pages 76–77. Sing the following song to the tune "Here We Go 'Round the Mulberry Bush":

Listen to the words I sing:
    *black, blue, blow; black, blue, blow;*
Now repeat the words with me:
    *black, blue, blow.*
Show the letters that start these words:
    *black, blue, blow; black, blue, blow;*
Then name some other words you know
    that start the same.

Children are to form the initial cluster, using the letter cards. Then invite them to name other words that begin with the cluster. These can be written on the board or Word Wall. Repeat the song, focusing on another consonant cluster.

## Blending Letters to Make Clusters

*Teacher Directed*

When reinforcing consonant clusters, use the following chart method.

1. Have children make large letter cards that form a consonant cluster you wish to reinforce. Example: $\boxed{b}$ $\boxed{l}$

2. Make a chart with three columns labeled *b*, *l*, and *bl* on the board or on chart paper. Write two familiar examples under each heading. Use action words for the consonant cluster column so that children will always associate a certain action with the cluster. You will be reviewing /b/*b* and /l/*l* while introducing /bl/*bl*.

| b | l | bl |
|-----|------|-------|
| bat | look | blink |
| box | like | blow |

3. After reading the chart words together, say new words that begin with *b*, *l*, or *bl*. Have children repeat each word and indicate in which column to write the word by holding up one or both of the letter cards. Ask a child with a correct response to tell you where to write the word on the chart. Children can help you spell the word. Use words such as *boy, blue, lap, ball, black, bloom, bit, last, leaf, block, blind, lion, blouse,* and *band* to fill the chart. Once the chart is finished, read the words in each column together. Follow a similar procedure to reinforce other consonant clusters. As children become more proficient, they can have their own charts to fill in.

Rigby Best Teachers Press
101 Ways... SV 141901885X

## Moving Right Along

*Teacher Directed*

When reinforcing the initial clusters, use action words as your examples. Children will remember and associate the consonant cluster with the action. Here are some examples:

| | | | | |
|---|---|---|---|---|
| *blow* | *breathe* | *creep* | *clap* | *drive* |
| *fly* | *frown* | *grab* | *skip* | *slither* |
| *smile* | *sniff* | *spin* | *stomp* | *trot* |

Use the words to sing the following action song to the tune of "Row, Row, Row Your Boat." Hold up letter cards, such as *s* and *k*, and have children name the action word. *(skip)* Insert the action word *skip* in each blank to sing and act out the song. Continue the song, using another initial cluster and action word.

_____, _____, _____ with me.
I will show you how.
You can _____ so easily.
Do it with me now!

## Action Track

*Independent*

Make copies of the Racetrack Game Board found on page 53. Fill in or have children fill in each blank with an action word that begins with a consonant cluster. **Two to four players** can use a numbered spinner, found on page 60, to move game markers along the board while naming and acting out the word landed on. Play until everyone has finished the race.

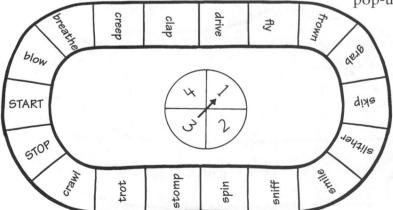

## Tongue Twister a Day

*Teacher Directed*

Tongue twisters are a great way to use a collection of words having a common consonant cluster. You may want to begin each day by saying a tongue twister and having children repeat it, saying it faster each time. Write the words on chart paper as children watch. A volunteer can underline initial clusters that are repeated. As you add to your chart each day, review some of the old tongue twisters. Invite children to say their favorites. Eventually children can create tongue twisters for the chart. Here are some examples:

- Blindfolded Blanche blew a blizzard of blue bubbles.
- Brandy's brother Brian brought brown bread for brunch.
- Grady Grocer groans when grouchy Greta grabs a group of green grapes.
- Flexible Floyd flips flat flapjacks.
- Sleepy Slick slipped on slippery slime in his slippers.

Children may want to publish tongue twisters they write, using the Pop-Up Book pattern from page 71. They can write the tongue twister on the cover and illustrate a picture to glue on the pop-up inside.

Flexible Floyd flips flat flapjacks.

# Cluster Word Wheels

Provide copies of the Word Wheel pattern on page 69. Show children how to cut out and assemble the wheels.
Model how to write a consonant cluster on the right side of the top wheel and add letters around the bottom wheel to form words.
Plan with children so that different clusters are represented on the wheels. In this way children can trade wheels to read.

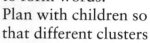

# Traveling Along

**Partners** can play a game to reinforce words with the final clusters *st, ft, nt, mp, nk, nd, ld, lk*. Use the S-Shape Game Board patterns found on pages 55–56. In each section, write a word that ends with a cluster and is associated with traveling through a town or city. Suggested words: *pavement, restaurant, ramp, hydrant, honk, sidewalk, bump, newsstand, playground, fast, left, lost, walk, dead end, find, went, trunk, bank, past, west, east, signpost, shift, gas pump, crank, bend, behind, wind*, and *child*. Players can use the numbered spinner, found on page 60, to determine the number of moves. They read the word landed on and name the letters that form the final cluster. Play until everyone has reached the *end of the road*. Use toy cars for playing pieces.

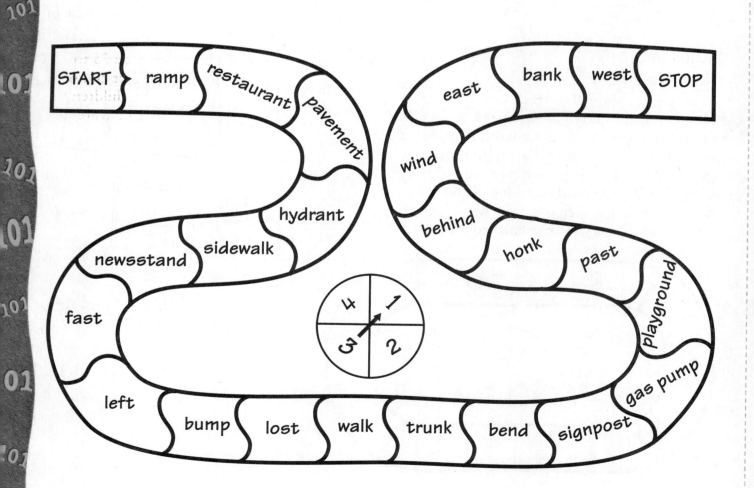

Rigby Best Teachers Press
101 Ways... SV 141901885X

# Activities for Consonant Digraphs

You can duplicate and send home School-Home Newsletter 5, page 46, to provide families with fun, easy-to-do activities for reinforcing consonant digraphs.

## Making Words with Digraphs

*Teacher Directed*

Provide copies of the individual Letter Cards and the Word Builder pattern from pages 76–78. Children can make words with single consonant beginnings and then move on to words beginning with digraphs. Example: First, have children make the word *in*. Then, have them add beginning consonants to form the words *fin, pin, tin,* and *win*. Continue by making four-letter words with beginning digraphs: *chin, shin, thin*. As words are made, have volunteers add them to a Word Wall.

Other word sets to form could be:

> *hip, rip, sip, tip, chip, ship, whip*
> *hop, mop, top, chop, shop*
> *heat, meat, seat, cheat, wheat*
> *lick, sick, tick, chick, thick*

**Partners** can work on their own to form other word groups and add these new groups to the Word Wall or individual word files.

## Sorting Out Words

*Independent*

Use index cards or the Word Cards pattern on page 75 to make packs of twenty-four word cards. In each pack, include words that begin with *c, ch, s, sh, t, th, w,* and *wh* (three of each). Choose words that can be sorted in various ways. Sample pack:

| | |
|---|---|
| cot, corn, cow | chow, chip, chop |
| seat, sick, sink | shin, ship, shop |
| ten, tin, top | thorn, thick, think |
| win, wink, worn | whip, when, wheat |

Allow children to figure out how they want to sort the words. After sorting one way, have them try another way. Words can be sorted by initial sounds; ending sounds; vowel sounds; words that rhyme; and three-, four-, and five-letter words. Provide blank cards for children to add more words to each sort.

## Beginning and Ending Sorts

*Independent*

Use the Word Cards pattern on page 75 to make cards with words that begin or end with the digraphs *sh, th,* and *ch*. Allow children to figure out how they want to sort the words. Words you might include:

*shell, shop, shoe, shirt, show, sheep, push, dish, wash, wish, sash, flash, fish, think, thank, thirty, thunder, thorn, thing, thick, thin, both, cloth, teeth, path, bath, with, math, fourth, chair, cheese, cheek, chalk, child, chin, cherry, chew, beach, catch, each, inch, lunch, march, much, reach, watch.*

Always ask children to read the words in each of their categories, and provide blank cards in case they want to add more words.

## Consonant Digraph Relay

*Teacher Directed*

Have children form **teams of four** members. Say a word that begins or ends with a digraph. Teammates take turns writing each letter of the word on the board, in order, until the word is complete. If a player makes a mistake, the next teammate can correct it. Play until all teams have finished the word. A point is scored for each correct spelling. Once children become more proficient, make this a timed race to see which team finishes first.

## Digraph Word Wheels

*Independent*

Have children cut out the blank Word Wheel from the pattern on page 69. Show them how to assemble the wheels. Then model how to write a digraph on the right side of the top wheel and add letters around the bottom wheel to form words. Plan with children so that different digraphs are represented on the wheels. In this way children can trade wheels to read.

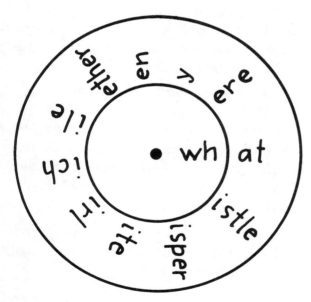

## Tongue Twister a Day, Part II

*Teacher Directed*

If children enjoyed using words with consonant clusters to create tongue twisters, follow a similar procedure for words with initial digraphs. Here are some examples to get you started:

- Charlie Champ cheerfully chomps chicken chili and chocolate cherry cheesecake.
- Shy Sheila sheared seven short shaggy sheep.
- Thankful Thelma threw a thimble on her throbbing thumb.

# Activities for
# R-Controlled Vowels

 You can duplicate and send home School-Home Newsletter 6, page 47, to provide families with fun, easy-to-do activities for reinforcing *r*-controlled vowels.

## Giant Tic-Tac-Toe

*Teacher Directed*

Select **nine children** to arrange their chairs in tic-tac-toe formation. Provide nine sheets of construction paper with a giant *X* on one side and a giant *O* on the other side. The remaining children form two teams—X's and O's. Alternate saying a word with an *r*-controlled vowel to members of each team. The player must say the word and spell it. Write the word on the board to verify. If correct, the team directs one of the nine children to hold up an *X* or an *O*, as appropriate. Play until one team wins or there is a tie. Follow the same procedure for another round. You can also use this game to focus on words with other phonic elements.

## Star Players

*Independent*

For each game, reproduce two copies of the 16-Square Grid from page 62. Use one copy as a game board that children can cover by drawing and coloring stars. Write words with the vowel-*r* pattern in the sections on the second copy, and cut apart the cards. To play, **partners** place the word cards face up on the game board to cover the stars. Players take turns choosing a word to read and asking the partner to find and remove the word from the game board. Play until all the words are gone so the stars show.

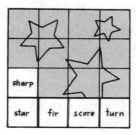

## Star Riddle Writers

*Independent*

Provide copies of the Pull-Out Book pattern on page 74. Model how to cut out and assemble the books. Then children write riddles about words containing an *r*-controlled vowel. The riddle can be written on the blank page with the answer hidden on the pull-out tab. Encourage children to include as many *r*-controlled words as possible in their writing. Here is a riddle to get them started:

This is a large fish with very sharp teeth. If you see its fin, hurry and start for the shore What is it?
*(a shark)*

# Activities for Vowel Diphthongs and Vowel Variants

 You can duplicate and send home School-Home Newsletter 7, page 48, to provide families with fun, easy-to-do activities for reinforcing vowel diphthongs and vowel variants.

## Vowel Cover-Up

### Independent

For each game, you will need the Dot Game Board and the Word Cards from pages 59 and 75. First, fill the dots with the vowel spellings *oo, au, aw, oi, oy, ow, ou,* and *ea.* Write words containing these vowels on the cards. To play, **partners** will turn the word cards facedown. They will take turns turning over a card to read and then finding and covering the vowel spelling on the game board. Players can use cotton balls, coins, or plastic markers to cover the dots. Play until all the words have been read and all the dots are covered.

## Sort and Split

### Independent

Use the Word Cards pattern on page 75 to make sets of cards with the words *launch, faucet, autumn, sauce, August, sausage, fawn, shawl, straw, hawk, lawn, draw, brown, down, plow, crown, flower, owl, house, mountain, cloud, sound, pouch,* and *blouse.* Children can work **independently or with a partner** to sort the words into two groups according to like vowel sounds (*au* and *aw* words / *ow* and *ou* words). Then have them split the words in each group again to form words with like spellings for those vowel sounds. (*au, aw/ow, ou*)

## Loop to Loop

### Independent

Use the Word Cards pattern from page 75 to make a set of cards with words containing the vowels *oi, oy, ow, ou, au, aw,* and *oo.* On each word card, write a numeral from 1 to 4. Use the cards with copies of the Loop Game Board from pages 57–58. Glue the loops together on a file folder to make the game board.

To begin play, stack the cards facedown. **Two or three players** take turns picking a card from the stack to read. If read correctly, the card is returned to the bottom of the stack, and the player moves a game marker the number of spaces indicated by the numeral on the word card. If the word is not identified, the player forfeits a move and must give the word card to the next player to read. Play until everyone has moved from loop to loop to the end of the path.

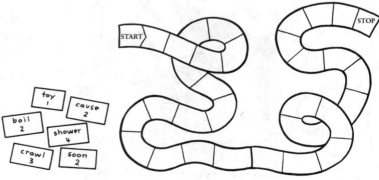

# Activities for Contractions

You can duplicate and send home School-Home Newsletter 8, page 49, to provide families with fun, easy-to-do activities for reinforcing contractions. It also includes activities for reinforcing possessives.

## We'll Be Coming 'Round the Mountain

*Independent*

Use copies of the Mountain Game Board from page 54. Write a contraction on half of the spaces and two words that can form a contraction on the other spaces. **Partners** choose one side of the mountain to begin play, starting at the bottom and taking turns climbing up one side and down the other. To move, they jump over one another, landing on every other word. If a player lands on a contraction, the two words forming the contraction should be identified and spelled. If two words are landed on, the player should say and spell the contraction that can be formed. Once players have reached the other side of the mountain, they can reverse to go back over again so that a new set of words is identified.

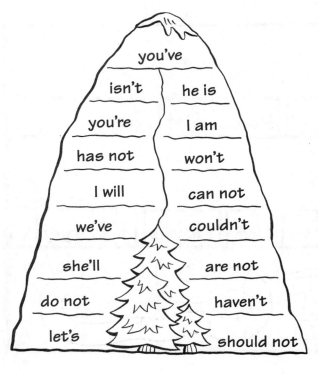

## Contraction Concentration

*Teacher Directed*

Write each of the following contractions and word pairs on large cards or sheets of paper: *didn't, did not, wasn't, was not, let's, let us, we'll, we will, they're, they are*. Give the cards to **ten volunteers** who will stand across the front of the room with the blank side of the card facing the group of players. The group will play a game of Concentration, with players taking turns asking two card holders to turn around their word cards. If a match between a contraction and corresponding word pair is made, the card holders stand off to the side. If a match is not made, the cards are turned around again. Play Concentration until all matches have been made. Make new cards for another game. **Individual** games can be made using Word Cards from page 75.

## Contraction Builders

*Teacher Directed*

Provide children with sets of Letter Cards and a Word Builder, found on pages 76–78. Blank cards can be used to make an apostrophe and additional letter cards that are needed. Children build pairs of words you say by placing the letter cards in the pocket of the Word Builder. Then have them replace one or more letters with an apostrophe to make the contraction that means the same. Use these words: *let us, was not, I am, has not, he is, you are, are not, is not, you have.*

# Activities for Possessives

You can duplicate and send home School-Home Newsletter 8, page 49, to provide families with fun, easy-to-do activities for reinforcing possessives. It also includes activities for reinforcing contractions.

## Silly Sentences with 's

*Teacher Directed*

Use silly alliterative sentences to reinforce and provide examples of names with the possessive form 's. Write examples on the board or on chart paper, and read them with children.

- Kevin's kangaroo kicked Karen's cousin Kyle.
- Luisa's load of lemons landed in Larry's lap.
- Papa will pay for Pepe's peck of pickled peppers and Polly's pound of peaches.
- Floyd's flapjacks flew and fell flat on Flora's flowerpot.

The sentences could be written on strips and the words then cut apart so that children can arrange them in a pocket chart. The words can be arranged in more than one way.

Have children write their silly sentences, and suggest that they publish them using the Step-Page Book pattern, page 72. Each child's sentence can be written on the first step, and classmates' sentences can be copied onto the other pages.

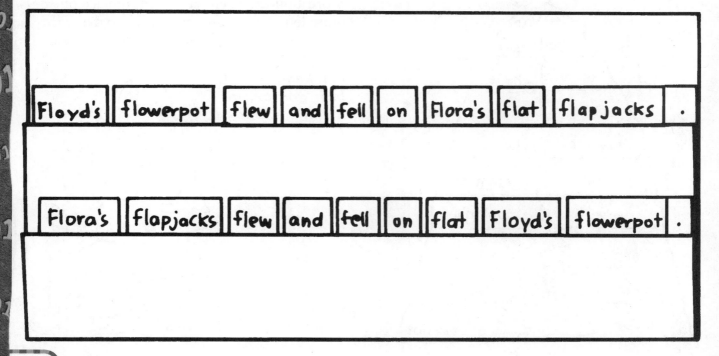

Rigby Best Teachers Press
101 Ways... SV 141901885X

# Activities for Inflected Endings

You can duplicate and send home School-Home Newsletter 9, page 50, to provide families with fun, easy-to-do activities for reinforcing inflected endings.

## Action Word Wall

One way to start or add to a Word Wall featuring words with inflected endings is to involve children in performing actions. Your Word Wall might be divided into four sections like this:

| base word | ending -s or -es | ending -ing | ending -ed |
|-----------|------------------|-------------|------------|
|           |                  |             |            |

Add words to the wall while using the word in context and having children demonstrate the action. Use a procedure like this: Ask who can *twirl*. Write the word *twirl* in the first column. Then tell children to watch as a volunteer *twirls*. Write the word *twirls* in the second column. As the child is moving, ask the group to name what he or she is doing. Write their response *twirling* in the third column. Once the child is seated, ask the group what the child did. Write *twirled* in the last column. When several words are on the wall, read them together and talk about the base words and the endings. For older children, you could include words that require spelling changes, such as *carry, carries, carrying, carried*.

## Wordo

Provide **each child** with a copy of the 16-Square Grid found on page 62 and game markers. Call on children to pick words from the Word Wall that will be included in the game. As each word is chosen, all players write the word in one space on their game sheet as you write it on an index card. All children will have the same words on their sheets but in different spaces. Once the sheets are filled, shuffle the cards and start to play. As each word is called, have children repeat the word, chant its spelling, and cover it on their sheets. Play until someone has covered all the words in a row.

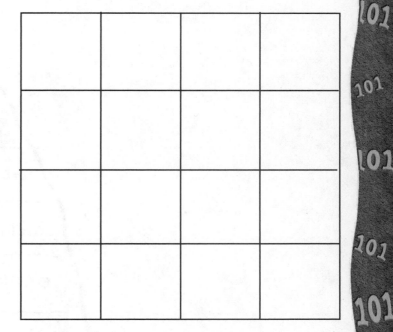

## Sort and Spell

*Independent*

Use the Word Cards pattern found on page 75 to make a set of base word cards to which inflected endings can be added. Include words such as *jump, carry, smile, run, stop, wash, hurry, copy, paint, sleep, chase, fix, skip, clap, bake, help, reach, splash, dance, erase, hum, plan, sneeze,* and *work*. First, have children sort the words into base words that require spelling changes when an ending is added and those that do not. (Spelling changes are required of words ending with *y* or *e* and most words ending with a single consonant.) Then, children can add *-s, -es, -ing,* or *-ed* to each word and write it on paper to verify.

## Hiking Up Word Mountain

*Independent*

Use copies of the Mountain Game Board found on page 54. In each space, write a word with the inflected ending *-s, -es, -ed,* or *-ing*, including words that require spelling changes. **Partners** choose one side of the mountain to begin play, starting at the bottom and taking turns climbing up one side and down the other. To move, they jump over one another, landing on every other word. They must read the word and spell the base word. Once players have reached the other side of the mountain, they should reverse to go back over again so that a new set of words is identified.

keeping

jumps — sees

stopped — glasses

catches — staring

smiles — hoped

waited — stomps

stepping — struggling

watches — carries

climbs — rested

# Activities for Prefixes

You can duplicate and send home School-Home Newsletter 10, page 51, to provide families with fun, easy-to-do activities for reinforcing prefixes. It also includes activities for reinforcing suffixes.

## Know and Don't-Know Sorts

**Independent**

Use the Word Cards pattern from page 75 to make a pack of cards with words having prefixes: *retell, unsafe, dislike, reload, unpack, disobey, rewrite, unable, distrust, refill, unclear, displease, repaint, unload, disappear, reuse, unroll, disagree, retie, unafraid, recheck, unbutton, dishonest, unhappy.* Children can read and sort the words according to the prefix. Then they can sort again into groups of words they can define and those they do not know. You may want to write the meaning on the back of each word card or provide an answer key.

## Run the Bases

**Teacher Directed**

Create a baseball diamond in the room, labeling home plate and first, second, and third base. Write words with suffixes on the board or have children refer to a Word Wall they have created. Then, children take turns standing at home plate to choose a word to read. They get to first base by reading the word, to second base by identifying the base word, to third base by defining the word, and to home plate by using the word in a sentence. Form **two teams** if children wish.

## A Game Board of Sorts

**Independent**

Make copies of the Loop Game Board pattern on pages 57–58. Use the blank spinner pattern, page 60, and divide it into three sections. Write the words *return, undo,* and *dislike* on the spinner. Fill the spaces on the game board with words beginning with *re-, un-,* and *dis-*. **Two or three players** take turns spinning the spinner and moving a marker along the game board until they reach the first word that begins with the same prefix as that shown on the spinner. Players must read the words along the way and use the word landed on in a sentence. Play until everyone has traveled the loops.

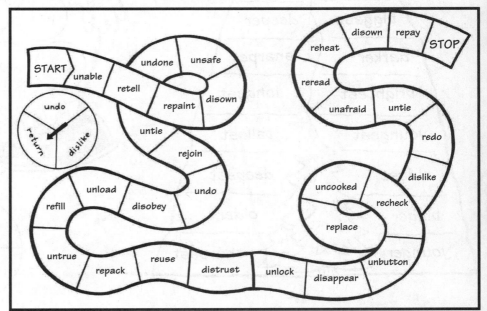

# Activities for Suffixes

You can duplicate and send home School-Home Newsletter 10, page 51, to provide families with fun, easy-to-do activities for reinforcing suffixes. It also includes activities for reinforcing prefixes.

## Climb the Highest Mountain

*Independent*

Make a copy of the Mountain Game Board found on page 54. In each section, write a word with the suffix *-er* or *-est*. **Partners** choose one side of the mountain to begin play, starting at the bottom and taking turns climbing up one side and down the other. To move, they jump over one another, landing on every other word. Players must read the word landed on and use it in a sentence to illustrate meaning. If the word is not identified, the partner can help out. Once players have reached the other side of the mountain, they should reverse to go back over again so that a new set of words is identified.

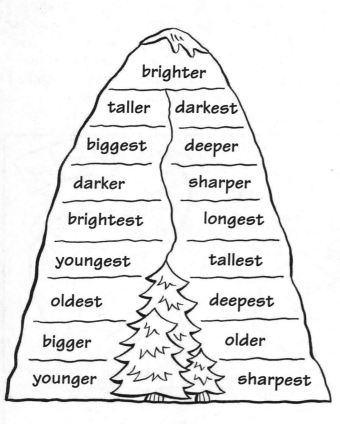

## Seeing Spots

*Independent*

Make a copy of the Dot Game Board found on page 59. On each dot, write a word that ends with a suffix, including *-er*, *-est*, *-ful*, *-less*, *-ness*, and *-ly*. Use the spinner pattern, page 60, and draw lines to make four sections. Write the numerals 1, 2, 1, 2 in the sections. **Partners** take turns spinning the spinner, reading one or two words, and naming and spelling the base words. As words are read, they can be covered with cotton balls or game markers. When all the words are covered, the partners may want to invite two more players to join them to spin, remove one or two markers at a time, and read the words.

Rigby Best Teachers Press
101 Ways... SV 141901885X

# Reproducible
# Phonics Resources

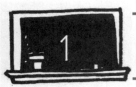 

# School ⟷ Home Newsletter

## Dear Family,

Your child has been learning about consonants. As your child continues to learn about consonant letters and the sounds they make in words, you can participate, too, by trying some activities at home. These activities will help your child become a better reader and writer.

## After-School Activities

Everyone's name has consonant letters in it. So do the names of things you use every day.

✓ Have your child write his or her name and circle all the consonant letters. See how many words your child can say that begin or end with each of those letters. Then help your child list the words. You can use books or a dictionary to find words, too.

Ⓜo Ⓝ i Ⓒ a

| | | |
|---|---|---|
| mud | nuts | cat |
| money | nose | car |
| mail | net | cow |
| hum | van | corn |

✓ Work together to think of the names of foods that begin with each consonant. Look in kitchen cupboards and recipe books for ideas. Make a book of the names. Draw a picture or cut a picture from a magazine to go with each food name. Then create menus in which all the foods must begin with the same consonant.

## Project Time

Fill an empty container with dirt or clay. Put a branch in the container so it stands up. Your child can cut paper leaves and write words on them that begin with consonants and name things that tell about the current season or an upcoming holiday. Read the words together.

### Phonics Focus

The letters *b, c, d, f, g, h, j, k, l, m, n, p, q, r, s, t, v, w, x, y,* and *z* are **consonants**.

✂ Cut out this bookmark and take it to the library.

### Get Into Books

Look for these alphabet books. Help your child notice the words that begin with consonants:

*Alphabears* by Kathleen Hague. Henry Holt and Company, 1984.

*Animalia* by Graeme Base. Harry N. Abrams, 1987.

*Dr. Seuss's ABC* by Dr. Seuss. Random House, 1963.

*Eating the Alphabet* by Lois Ehlert. Harcourt, 1993.

*What Pete Ate from A to Z* by Maira Kalman. Putnam, 2001.

Rigby Best Teachers Press
101 Ways... SV 141901885X

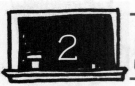 

# 2 School ←→ Home Newsletter

## Dear Family,

Your child has been learning about words with short vowel sounds. As your child continues to learn about vowel sounds and the letters that spell these sounds, you can participate, too, by trying some activities at home.

## After-School Activities

Use the names of items found in your home to give your child practice with reading and writing words with short vowel sounds.

✓ Invite your child to go on a scavenger hunt. Write a list of things for your child to find, and read it together. If your child needs extra help, draw a picture of each thing. Here are some things to find:

| | | |
|---|---|---|
| hat | bell | big pan |
| toy | sock | ten spoons |
| nut | jam | six rocks |

✓ Read the words on your list aloud, and ask your child to say another word that rhymes with the name of each thing found. For example, *cat* rhymes with *hat*.

## Project Time

The word *map* has a short *a* in it. Give your child a large sheet of paper or a paper bag that has been cut and opened. Ask your child to draw a room map showing his or her bedroom and the things in it. Have your child label things that have names with short vowels, such as the *bed, desk, rug,* and *clock.*

## Phonics Focus

The letters *a, e, i, o,* and *u* are **vowels.** The words *cat, bed, six, box,* and *cup* have **short vowel** sounds. If a short word or a syllable in a longer word has only one vowel and it is positioned between two consonants, the vowel is likely to have a short vowel sound as in the words above.

 Cut out this bookmark and take it to the library.

## Get Into Books

Look for these books that feature words with short vowel sounds:

*Hello, Cat, You Need a Hat* by Rita G. Gelman. Scholastic, 1999. short *a*

*Better Not Get Wet, Jesse Bear* by Nancy White Carlstrom. Simon & Schuster, 1988. short *e*

*Zin Zin Zin a Violin* by Lloyd Moss. Simon & Schuster, 1995. short *i*

*Fox in Socks* by Dr. Seuss. Random House, 1965. short *o*

*Thump and Plunk* by Janice May Udry. HarperCollins, 1981. short *u*

# School ←→ Home Newsletter

## Dear Family,

Your child has been learning about words with long vowel sounds. As your child continues to learn about vowel sounds and the letters that spell these sounds, you can participate, too, by trying some activities at home. These activities will help your child become a better reader and writer.

## After-School Activities

Do you recycle? What kinds of things do you use again—boxes, cans, glass jars, plastic containers, toys, or clothing?

✓ Help your child recycle word parts. Write the following word parts on paper. Help your child make as many words as possible by adding different beginning letters and saying the words aloud.

| | | | |
|---|---|---|---|
| _ain | _ame | _ale | _one |
| _eet | _ite | _eam | _ide |
| _ight | _oat | _oke | _ube |

Help your child write them on small separate pieces of paper. Sort the words according to vowel sound and put them in separate bags.

✓ Use the words from one bag to play a guessing game. Give clues about a word and have your child guess the word. Then your child can take a turn. Example: "I'm thinking of a word that has the sound of long *a*, and it names the water that falls from the clouds."

## Phonics Focus

The letters *a, e, i, o,* and *u* are **vowels**. The words *cake, leaf, bike, boat,* and *flute* have **long vowel** sounds. There are different ways to spell long vowels, such as with one letter as in *me*, with two letters as in *meet*, or with a vowel and final *e* as in *bake*.

 Cut out this bookmark and take it to the library.

## Get Into Books

Look for these great books that feature words with long vowel sounds:

*Jake Baked the Cake* by B. G. Hennessy. Penguin, 1990.

*Sheep in a Jeep* by Nancy Shaw. Houghton Mifflin, 1997.

*Mice Twice* by Joseph Low. Simon & Schuster, 1980.

*Moses Supposes His Toeses Are Roses* by Nancy Patz. Harcourt, 1981.

*Rude Giants* by Audrey Woods. Harcourt, 1998.

## Project Time

Help your child recycle newspapers, magazines, and junk mail by cutting out interesting words with long vowel sounds. Create a sign, a poster, a greeting card, or a message using the words.

  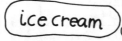 

Rigby Best Teachers Press
101 Ways... SV 141901885X

# School ⟷ Home Newsletter

## Dear Family,

Your child has been learning about the sounds of consonant clusters in words and the letters that form them. As your child continues to learn about consonant clusters, you can participate, too, by trying some activities at home. These activities will help your child become a better reader and writer.

## After-School Activities

What is the weather forecast for today? Your child can learn about weather while reading and writing words that have consonant clusters.

✓ Give your child three paper plates or sheets of paper to label with these words: *sunny weather, snowy weather, rainy weather*. Write the following words on small self-stick notes: *black clouds, freezing rain, sunglasses, damp, sled, clear blue sky, floods, ski-slope, warm front, gray skies, snowflakes, swimming, raindrops, sleet, sand, swings, cold front, mild breeze, wool gloves, summer camp, scarf, bright sunshine, plants grow, strong wind, ice skating.* Together read the words and underline the consonant clusters. Your child can stick each word on the paper plate that names the weather associated with it.

  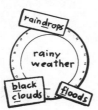

## Project Time

Your child might want to write a weather forecast for the following day. He or she can tell what the sky will look like, predict the high and low temperatures for the day, and describe any other weather conditions. See how many words with consonant clusters are used.

## Phonics Focus

A **consonant cluster** is two or three consonants that are blended together at the beginning or end of a word. The sound of each letter is heard. Consonant clusters found at the beginning of words include *br, cr, dr, fr, gr, pr, tr, bl, cl, fl, gl, pl, sl, sp, sk, st, sc, sl, sm, sn, sw, str, scr, squ,* and *thr*. Some clusters found at the end of words are *st, ft, nt, lk, lt, ld, mp, nd,* and *pt*.

**Cut out this bookmark and take it to the library.**

## Get Into Books

Look for these books that feature words with consonant clusters:

*In the Small, Small Pond* by Denise Fleming. Henry Holt, 1993. initial clusters with *s*

*There's a Nightmare in My Closet* by Mercer Mayer. Puffin, 1992. initial clusters with *l*

*Cloudy with a Chance of Meatballs* by Judi Barrett. Macmillan, 1978. variety of initial clusters

*Starring First Grade* by Miriam Cohen. Greenwillow, 1985. final clusters with *t*

*The Milk Makers* by Gail Gibbons. Macmillan, 1985. final cluster *lk*

*The Grumpalump* by Sarah Hayes. Clarion, 1991. final clusters *mp, nd*

# School ←→ Home Newsletter

## Dear Family,

Your child has been learning about words with consonant digraphs. As your child continues to learn about digraphs, you can participate, too, by trying some activities at home.

## After-School Activities

Ask your child to name the five senses. Then use <u>seeing</u>, <u>smelling</u>, <u>touching</u>, <u>hearing</u>, and <u>tasting</u> to help your child learn more about words that begin and end with consonant digraphs.

✓ On paper or a small chalkboard, write the following words that contain digraphs: *shop, lunch, quilt, chew, photo, sting, watch, whipped, skunk, thorn, thumb.* Read the words together, and have your child find and underline the letters that spell the digraph in each word: *sh, ch, qu, ch, ph, ng, tch, wh, nk, th, th-mb.*

✓ Play a guessing game using the words from above in questions like these:
  • What do you smell when you go in a bake *shop*?
  • What do you taste when you eat your favorite *lunch*?
  • How do you feel when you snuggle under a *quilt*?
  • What do you hear when you *chew* celery and carrot sticks?
  • Whom would you see in a *photo* of your friends?
  • What do you feel if you get a bee *sting*?
  • What do you hear when you listen to a *watch*?
  • What do you taste when you eat *whipped* potatoes?
  • What do you smell if a *skunk* gets scared?
  • What do you feel if a *thorn* pricks your *thumb*?

## Project Time

The words *chocolate chips, chewy,* and *crunchy* have the *ch* digraph. Look in a favorite recipe book for a dessert that fits that description, and ask your child to be a dessert chef by helping you make it for an after-dinner treat. Ask family members how it tastes.

## Phonics Focus

A **consonant digraph** in a word is two consonants together that stand for one unique sound. A digraph may begin or end a word, as in these examples: <u>sh</u>ip, fi<u>sh</u>, <u>wh</u>eel, <u>th</u>ink, ba<u>th</u>, <u>ph</u>one, laug<u>h</u>, <u>wr</u>ite, <u>kn</u>ow, <u>gn</u>aw, <u>ch</u>ew, crun<u>ch</u>, si<u>ng</u>, ba<u>nk</u>, <u>qu</u>een. The consonants *tch* form a three-letter digraph, as in the word *watch*.

Cut out this bookmark and take it to the library.

## Get Into Books

Look for these books featuring words with digraphs:

*The Quilt* by Ann Jonas. Greenwillow, 1984.  *qu*

*Is This a House for Hermit Crab?* by Megan McDonald. Orchard, 1990.  *ch, tch*

*Sheep on a Ship* by Nancy Shaw. Houghton Mifflin, 1989.  *sh, wh*

*The Fish Who Could Wish* by John Bush and Corky Paul. Kane-Miller, 1991.  *sh, wh*

*Elmer* by David McKee. Lothrop, 1989.  /f/ *gh, ph*

*Lionel in the Spring* by Stephen Krensky. Dial, 1990.  *ng, nk*

*Agatha's Feather Bed* by Carmen Agra Deedy. Peachtree, 1991.  variety of digraphs

# School ⟷ Home Newsletter

## Dear Family,

Your child has been learning about words in which the letter *r* gives the vowel a new sound. As your child continues to learn about *r*-controlled vowels, you can participate, too, by trying some activities at home.

## After-School Activities

Do you live in the city or the country? Use words that tell about these two places to help your child read and write words that have vowels with *r*.

✓ Make a category game. Write these words on small pieces of paper: *farm, corn, deer, garden, curbs, barn, herd, park, steer, birds, yard, turkey, fair, cart, bear, squirrel, circus, cable cars, horse, burro, turtle, sports arena, sheep shearing*. Help your child read the words, and categorize them into <u>city things</u> and <u>country things</u>. Do some of the words fit both categories?

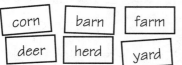 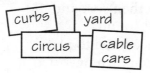

✓ Choose one group of words to tell or write a story together, using as many words as possible.

## Project Time

Have your child color or paint a city scene or a country scene, including pictures of some of the categorized words from the activities. When your child has finished, ask her or him to tell you about the picture and label the details, using words with a vowel + *r*.

## Phonics Focus

In some words, the letter *r* gives the vowel a new sound. The spellings of these **r-controlled vowels** include *ar, er, ir, or, ur, air, ear, eer, ore, our, oor,* and *oar*. Help your child notice words with these vowels and the sounds they make as you read and write together.

 Cut out this bookmark and take it to the library.

## Get Into Books

Look for these books that feature words with *r*-controlled vowels:

*Watch Out, Ronald Morgan!* by Patricia Reilly Giff. Viking, 1985.
words with *ear, eer*

*Farmer Goff and His Turkey Sam* by Brian Schatell. Lippincott, 1982.
words with *ar, ur, air, ear*

*Farm Noises* by Jane Miller. Simon & Schuster, 1992.
words with *ar*

*Garden in the City* by Gerda Muller. Dutton, 1992.
words with *ar*

*The Wednesday Surprise* by Eve Bunting. Clarion, 1989.
words with *er, ur*

*The Lady and the Spider* by Faith McNulty. HarperCollins, 1986.
words with *or, ore, our*

# 7 School ←→ Home Newsletter

## Dear Family,

Your child has been learning about words with vowel pairs. These vowel pairs have special spellings and stand for unique sounds. As your child continues to learn about vowel sounds and letters that stand for the sounds, you can try these activities at home.

## After-School Activities

Take a close look at words with special vowel pairs. Discover the fun and games suggested by some of these words.

✓ Write these words on separate cards or pieces of paper to create a sorting game:

> *yawn, lawn, taught, caught, thought, bought*
> *glue, blue, drew, chew*
> *coil, foil, soy, toy*
> *cow, now, out, shout*
> *could, should, would, book, cook, look*

Ask your child to read the words and then sort and stack words that have the same vowel sound.

✓ Mix the word cards and place them facedown to play a game of Concentration. Your child can turn over two cards at a time to read. If the words rhyme and have the same vowel spelling, the pair can be removed. If they do not, turn the cards facedown again.

## Project Time

How about having some outdoor fun? Some words that have vowel pairs suggest things you might do.

- *Draw* chalk pictures or a hopscotch game on the sidewalk or driveway.
- Play a game of tag or other running game on the *lawn*.
- Plan a family *cookout* with your favorite foods.
- Make up water *shower* games using empty dishwashing liquid bottles. They are great for squirting targets and people!
- Lie on the *ground* and find shapes in the *clouds*.

## Phonics Focus

In some words, two vowels appear together and stand for a special sound. In the words *saw, launch*, and *thought*, the vowel pairs *aw, au*, and *ou(gh)* stand for the same sound. In the words *clue* and *new*, the vowel sounds are the same but are spelled *ue* and *ew*. The vowels *ou* in *should* and *oo* in *brook* sound the same. These special vowel pairs are called **vowel variants**.

Vowel pairs *oi* and *oy* sound the same in *coin* and *toy*. The *ow* and *ou* in *cow* and *out* sound the same, too. These vowel pairs are called **diphthongs**.

 Cut out this bookmark and take it to the library.

## Get Into Books

Look for these books featuring words with vowel variants and diphthongs:

*The Luckiest Kid on the Planet* by Lisa Campbell Ernst. Bradbury, 1994. *ue, ew*

*The Monkey and the Crocodile* by Paul Galdone. Clarion, 1987. *aw, au, ou*

*Green Eggs and Ham* by Dr. Seuss. Random House, 1960. *oo, ou*

*Too Much Noise* by Ann McGovern. Houghton Mifflin, 1992. *oi, oy*

Rigby Best Teachers Press
101 Ways... SV 141901885X

# School ←→ Home Newsletter

## Dear Family,

Your child has been learning about using an apostrophe in words. As your child continues to discover how to use an apostrophe to write contractions and possessive forms of words, you can participate, too, by trying some activities at home.

## After-School Activities

Contractions and possessive forms of words are used every day in your conversations. Here are some ideas to help your child read and write these words.

✓ Ask your child what a *shortcut* is. Talk about shortcuts that can be taken to go to school, to a nearby store, or to a friend's house. See if your child recognizes word shortcuts called **contractions**. Make a matching game by writing the following on paper or on a small chalkboard:

| | | | |
|---|---|---|---|
| **don't** | I will | **you've** | I have |
| **you're** | let us | **we'd** | we would |
| **I'll** | do not | **they're** | you have |
| **let's** | you are | **I've** | they are |

Your child can read the words and draw lines to match each contraction to the words it stands for. Then read a book together and look for contractions that the writer used.

✓ Have your child ask to borrow one favorite thing owned by each family member. Place the items on a table. Help your child make signs to show who owns what, using the possessive form of each person's name.

## Project Time

Provide construction paper and help your child figure out how to make fancy place cards and napkin holders for your family dinner table, using the possessive form of names to mark each person's place.

## Focus on Word Structure

A **contraction** is a short way of writing two words as one word. An **apostrophe** replaces the one or more letters that are left out. Here are some examples:
*did not = didn't, I am = I'm, we will = we'll.*

An apostrophe is also used in **possessives** to show ownership. Use *'s* to show that something belongs to one person, animal, or thing: *the girl's bike.*

 Cut out this bookmark and take it to the library.

## Get Into Books

Look for these books that feature words with apostrophes:

*Where's My Teddy?* by Jez Alborough. Candlewick, 1992.
contractions

*"I Can't" Said the Ant* by Polly Cameron. Coward, McCann, 1961.
contractions

*I'm the Best!* by Marjorie Weinman Sharmat. Holiday House, 1991.
contractions

*Moonbear's Friend* by Frank Asch. Simon & Schuster, 1993.
possessives

*The Day Jimmy's Boa Ate the Wash* by Trinka Hakes Noble. Dial, 1980.
possessives

# School ⟷ Home Newsletter

## Dear Family,

Your child has been learning about endings that can be added to words to make new words. As your child continues to learn about words and their endings, you can participate, too, by trying some activities at home.

## After-School Activities

Numbers and time influence what we do every day. Help your child connect counting and time to learning about words with endings.

✓ Visit your local library and ask the librarian to help you find counting books. Some are listed on the bookmark. As you read the counting books with your child, look for words that mean more than one. Have your child spell some of the words aloud and notice whether the ending -s or -es was added.

✓ Model using words that tell about the present and the past (words with the endings -s, -ing, -ed). For example, you might pull out the family photo album and talk about what is happening in the photos, occasionally prompting "Remember when you . . ." Listen to the words your child is using.

## Focus on Word Structure

The **endings** -s, -es, -ing, and -ed can be added to words to make new words. The endings -s and -es are added to make a word mean "more than one," such as *dogs* and *foxes*. The endings -s, -es, and -ing are added to an action word to tell about something that is happening now: *runs, fixes, helping*. The ending -ed is added to an action word to tell about a past action: *worked*.

 Cut out this bookmark and take it to the library.

## Get Into Books

Look for these books that feature words with endings:

*Count-a-Saurus*
 by Nancy Blumenthal.
 Macmillan, 1989.  -s

*Counting Sheep*
 by John Archambault.
 Henry Holt, 1989.  -s, -es

*Who Wants One?* by Mary Serfozo.
 Margaret McElderry, 1989.
 -s, -es

*The Silly Tail Book* by Marc Brown.
 Parents Magazine Press, 1983.
 -s, -ing

*Walking Through the Jungle* by
 Julie Lacome. Candlewick, 1993.
 -ed, -ing

## Project Time

Do you have a special relative or family friend who lives far away? Ask your child to make a decorative greeting card or stationery. Work together to write a letter to this person, telling about things you have done. Then, reread the letter and check the spelling of words with endings.

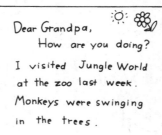

Dear Grandpa,
 How are you doing?
I visited Jungle World at the zoo last week. Monkeys were swinging in the trees.

# School ⟷ Home Newsletter

10

## Dear Family,

Your child has been learning about words with prefixes and suffixes. As your child continues to learn about word parts and their meanings, you can participate, too, by trying some activities at home.

## After-School Activities

Do you plant a garden at home? What must you do to make your garden grow? Tell your child that words can grow, too—when a prefix or a suffix is added, that is!

✓ After sharing a book with your child, go back and together look for words that have prefixes, such as *re-, dis-, pre-,* and *un-,* and suffixes, such as *-ful, -ness, -ly, -er, -est, -less,* and *-y.* Read the words and ask your child to name the word to which the prefix or suffix was added.

✓ Your child can make each of these words grow by adding the suffix *-ful: spoon, cup, mouth, hand, plate.* Then use the words to make up sentences related to eating and cooking. Here are a few more words with prefixes to use in sentences about cooking or kitchen appliances: *preheat, precooked, reheat, refreeze, disconnect, unload, refill, reuse, remove.*

## Project Time

Make word flowers to show how words grow by adding a prefix or a suffix. Cut circles and petal shapes from construction paper. Write a prefix or a suffix on a circle shape. Your child will write words that contain that prefix or suffix on the petals.
Use books or a dictionary to look for words. Glue the petals to the circle to form a flower. Add a pipe cleaner stem and paper leaves.

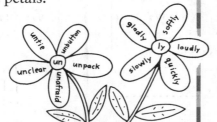

## Focus on Word Structure

A **suffix** is a word part added to the end of a base word to make a new word and change the meaning. Some suffixes are *-ful, -ness, -ly, -er, -est, -less,* and *-y.* A **prefix** is a word part added to the beginning of a base word to make a new word and change the meaning. Some prefixes are *re-, un-, dis-,* and *pre-.*

✂ Cut out this bookmark and take it to the library.

## Get Into Books

Look for these books that feature words with prefixes and suffixes:

*The Bad Dream* by Jim Aylesworth. Whitman, 1985.
suffixes *-ful, -ly*

*The Story of Jumping Mouse: A Native American Legend* retold by John Steptoe. Lothrop, 1984.
suffixes *-ful, -ly*

*Learning to Swim in Swaziland* by Nila K. Leigh. Scholastic, 1993.
suffixes *-ly, -y*

Better Homes and Gardens *Step-by-Step Kid's Cookbook.* Meredith Press, 1984.
prefixes and suffixes

*Mufaro's Beautiful Daughters* by John Steptoe. Lothrop, 1987.
prefixes and suffixes

 # School ←→ Home Newsletter

**Dear Family,**

## Phonics Focus

## After-School Activities

You may want to try these activities at home.

 Cut out this bookmark and take it to the library.

## Get Into Books

**Project Time**

Rigby Best Teachers Press
101 Ways... SV 141901885X

# Racetrack Game Board

1. Make two copies.   2. Cut out.   3. Glue onto a file folder.

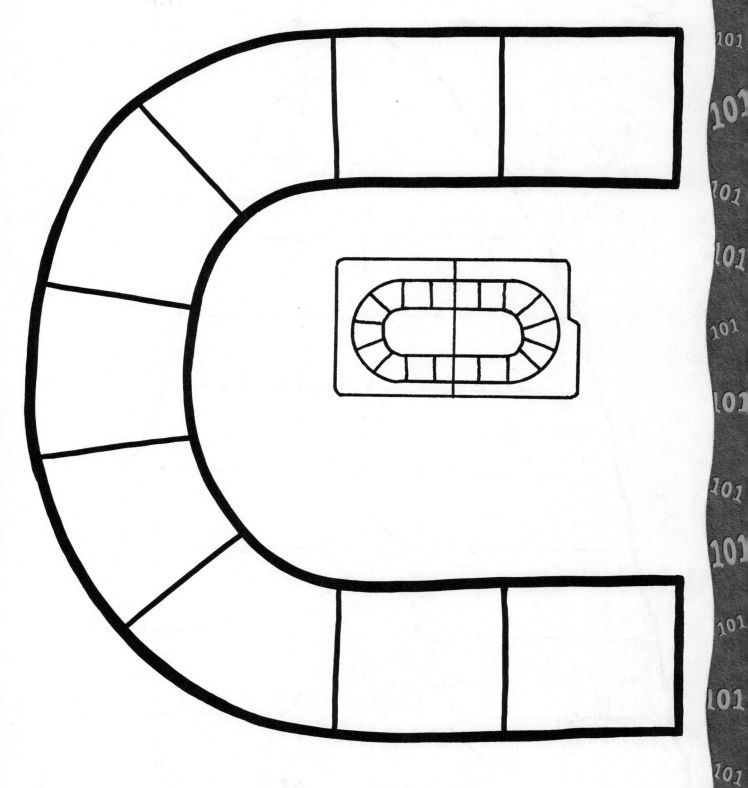

Rigby Best Teachers Press
101 Ways... SV 141901885X

www.harcourtschoolsupply.com

# Mountain Game Board

## 1. Cut out.    2. Glue onto construction paper.

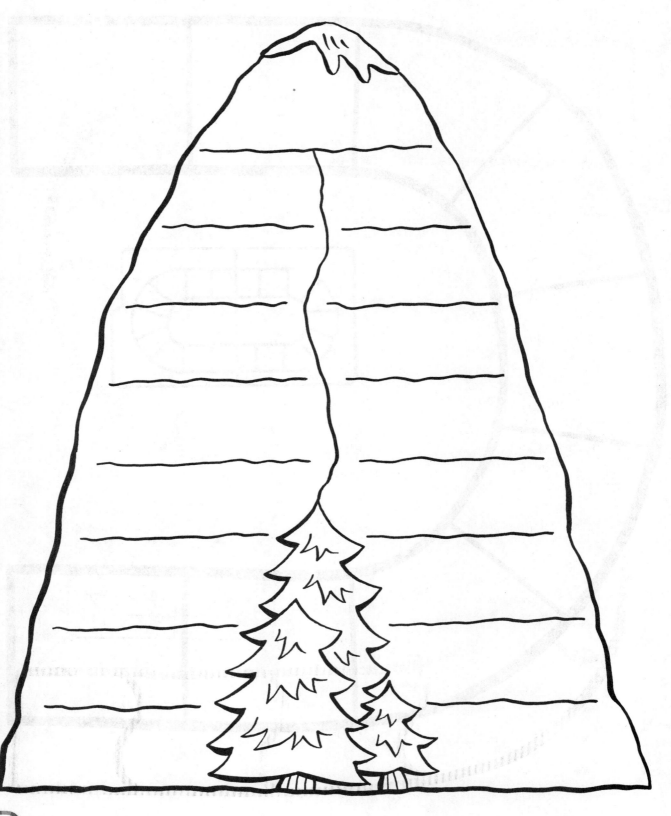

Rigby Best Teachers Press
101 Ways... SV 141901885X

# S-Shape Game Board (left side)

## 1. Make a copy of both S-Shape Game Boards. 2. Cut out.
## 3. Glue onto a file folder.

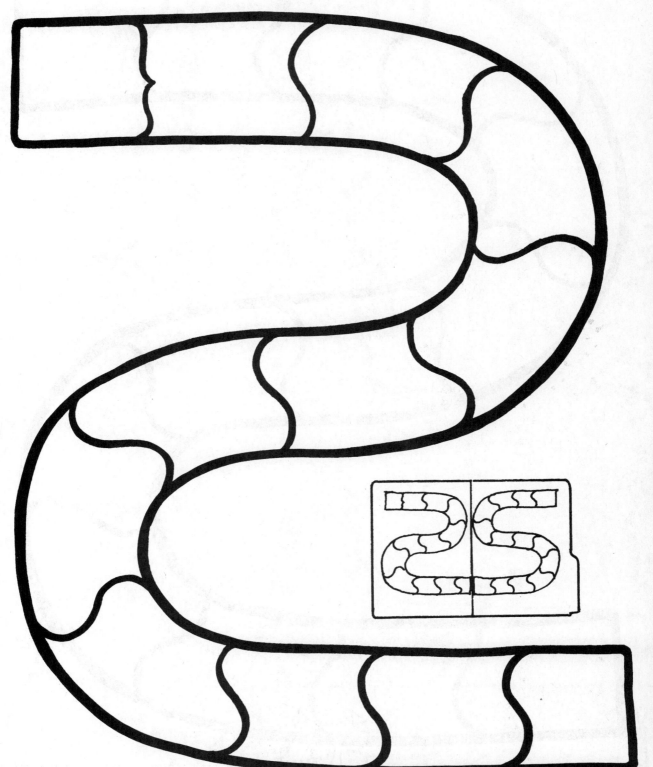

Rigby Best Teachers Press
101 Ways... SV 141901885X

www.harcourtschoolsupply.com

# S-Shape Game Board (right side)

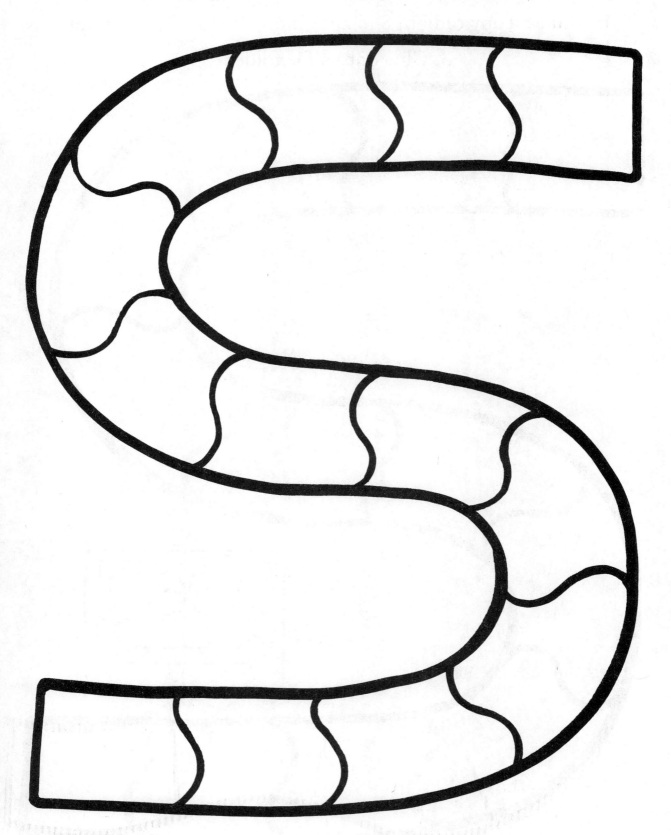

Rigby Best Teachers Press
101 Ways... SV 141901885X

# Loop Game Board (left side)

1. Make a copy of both Loop Game Boards.    2. Cut out.

3. Glue onto a file folder.

*Rigby Best Teachers Press*
101 Ways... SV 141901885X

www.harcourtschoolsupply.com

# Loop Game Board (right side)

Rigby Best Teachers Press
101 Ways... SV 141901885X

# Dot Game Board

## 1. Cut out.  2. Glue onto construction paper.

# Spinners

1. Cut out a wheel and glue it onto thick paper.
2. Put on a paper clip with a brad.

**Blank Spinner**

www.harcourtschoolsupply.com
© Harcourt Achieve Inc. All rights reserved.

Rigby Best Teachers Press
101 Ways... SV 141901885X

# 9-Square Grid

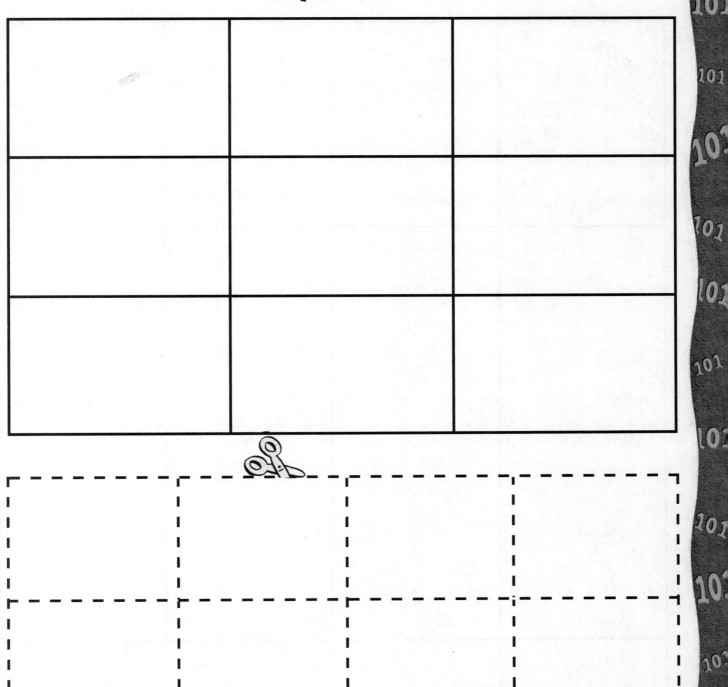

# 16-Square Grid

Rigby Best Teachers Press
101 Ways... SV 141901885X

# Finger Puppets

1. Cut.

2. Draw or write.

3. Tape.

4. Wear.

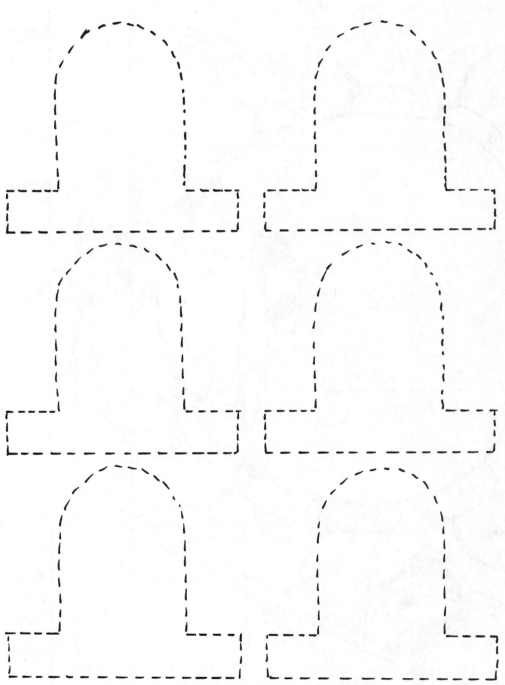

*Rigby Best Teachers Press*
101 Ways... SV 141901885X

www.harcourtschoolsupply.com

# Crab Word Slide

Cut out the strip. Write a word with short *a* in each box.
The crab will give you ideas. Cut the slits on the crab.
Pull the strip and read the words.

Rigby Best Teachers Press
101 Ways... SV 141901885X

# Hen Word Slide

Cut out the strip. Write a word with short *e* in each box.
The hen will give you ideas. Cut the slits on the hen.
Pull the strip and read the words.

# Pig Word Slide

Cut out the strip. Write a word with short *i* in each box. The pig will give you ideas. Cut the slits on the pig. Pull the strip and read the words.

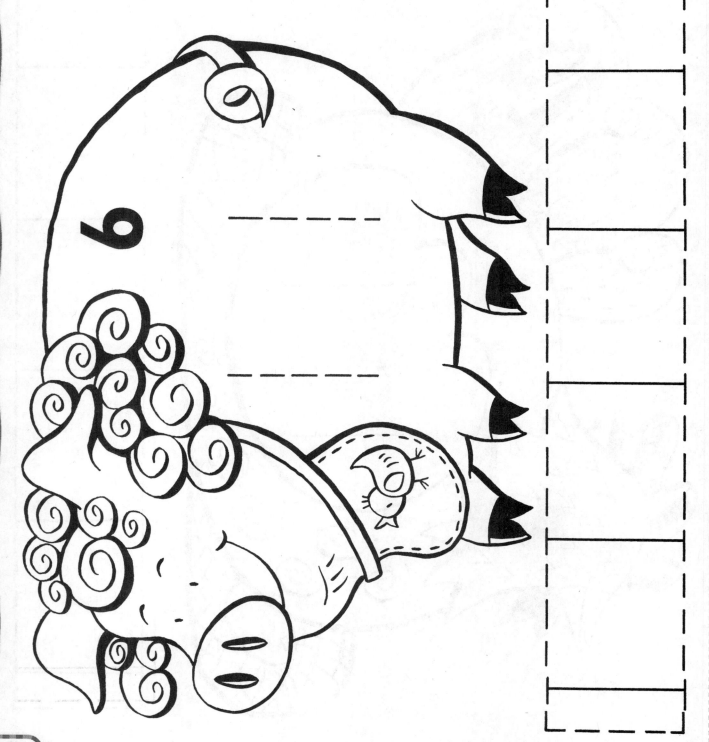

Rigby Best Teachers Press
101 Ways... SV 141901885X

# Fox Word Slide

Cut out the strip. Write a word with short *o* in each box. The fox will give you ideas. Cut the slits on the fox. Pull the strip and read the words.

# Bug Word Slide

Cut out the strip. Write a word with short *u* in each box. The bug will give you ideas. Cut the slits on the bug. Pull the strip and read the words.

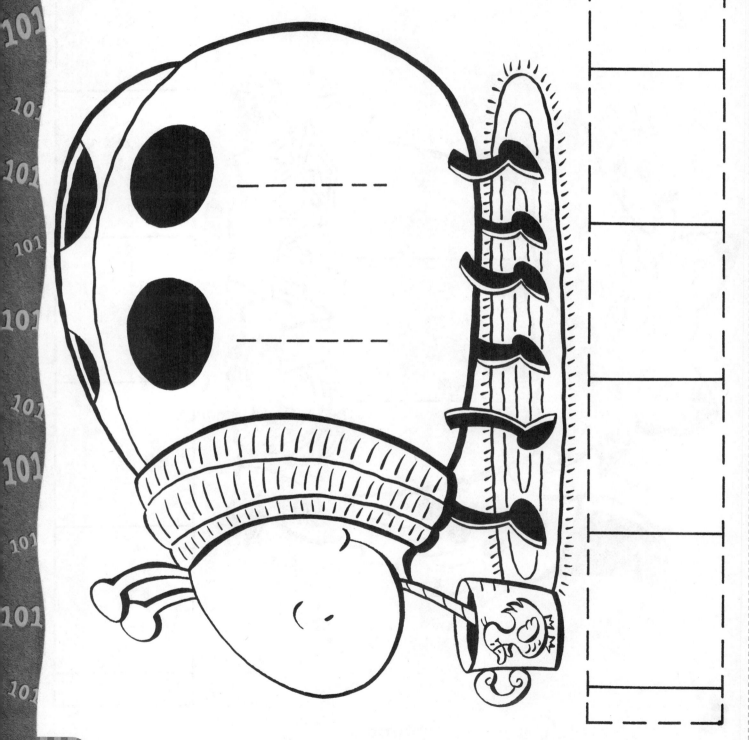

Rigby Best Teachers Press
101 Ways... SV 141901885X

# Word Wheel

## 1. Cut out each wheel.   2. Attach with a brad.

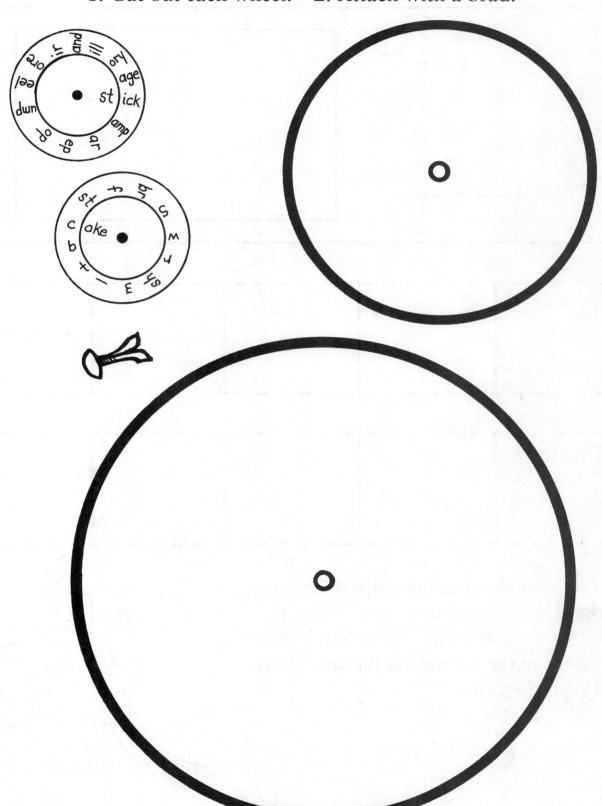

# Wordscope

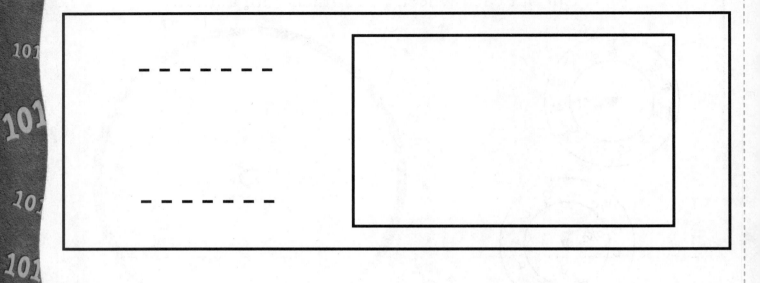

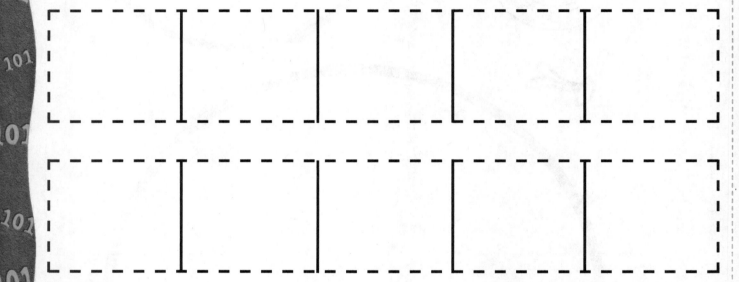

Cut out the box and the strips. Cut slits in the box on the dotted lines. Write a phonogram in the box. Write letters that stand for initial sounds on the strip. Pull and read the words.

# Pop-Up Book

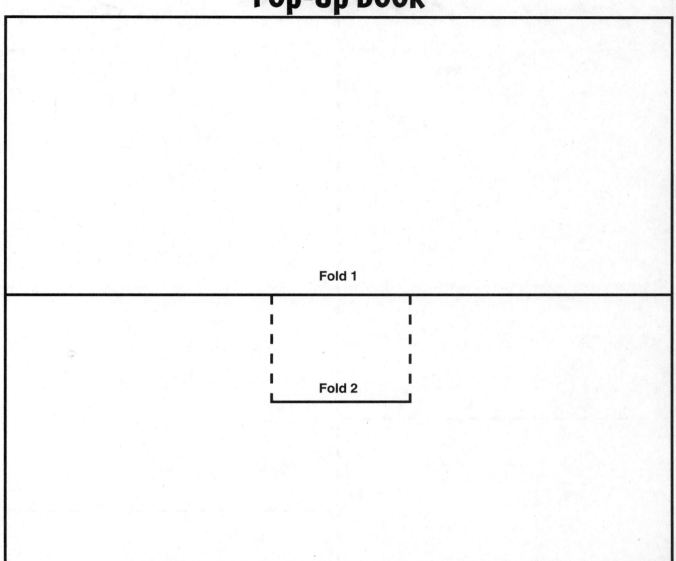

**Fold 1**

**Fold 2**

1. Cut out the book. Fold the book in half.

2. Cut on the dotted lines through both layers.

3. Fold on the solid lines. Open and refold so the box will pop out.

4. Glue it inside a cover.

5. Glue a picture on the pop-up.

Rigby Best Teachers Press
101 Ways... SV 141901885X

www.harcourtschoolsupply.com

# Step-Page Book

1. Cut out the four pages.

2. Lay the pages one on top of the other.

3. Bind the pages at the top.

Rigby Best Teachers Press
101 Ways... SV 141901885X

# Flip Book

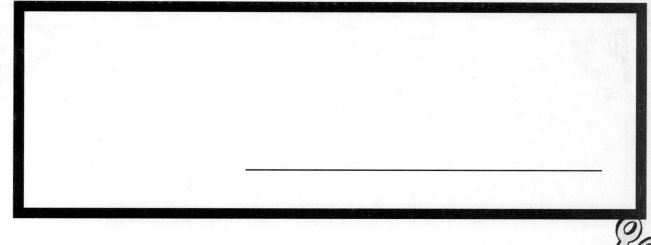

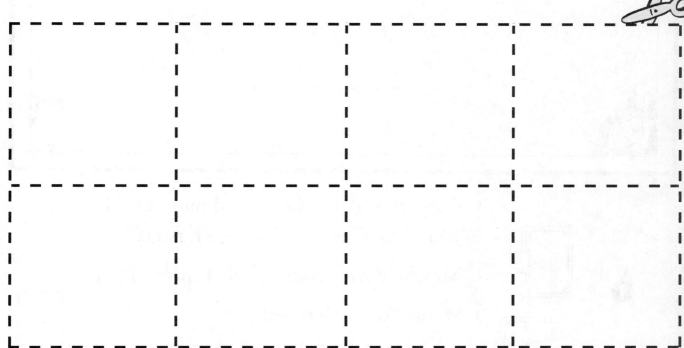

Cut out the book back and the pages. Write a phonogram on the right side of the book back. Write letters that stand for beginning sounds on the pages. Staple the pages to the book back. Flip the pages to read the words.

**Rigby Best Teachers Press**
101 Ways... SV 141901885X

www.harcourtschoolsupply.com

# Pull-Out Book

- - - - - - - - - -

**1.** ○ 1. Cut out as many pages and pull-out tabs as you need. Cut the slit on each page.

**2.** ○ 2. Make a cover from a folded sheet of paper.

**3.** ○ 3. Staple the book together.

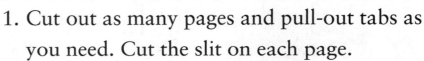

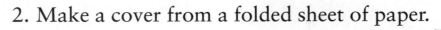

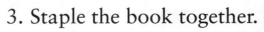

Pull

**Rigby Best Teachers Press**
101 Ways... SV 141901885X

# Word Cards

Rigby Best Teachers Press
101 Ways... SV 141901885X

www.harcourtschoolsupply.com

# Letter Cards (Lowercase)

a b c d e

f g h i j

k l m n o

p q r s t

u v w x y

z

Rigby Best Teachers Press
101 Ways... SV 141901885X

# Letter Cards (Uppercase)

A B C D E

F G H I J

K L M N O

P Q R S T

U V W X Y

Z

Rigby Best Teachers Press
101 Ways... SV 141901885X

www.harcourtschoolsupply.com

# Word Builder

1. Cut out the Word Builder.

2. Fold up the pocket.

3. Staple it on each side.

4. Draw an arrow
   on the pocket.

Fold. ⬑

Rigby Best Teachers Press
101 Ways... SV 141901885X

# Reading Log

_____
(name)

Keeping Track
of Reading

Book Title _____

Author _____

What did you think of the book? _____

_____

_____

_____

Tape the cars together. Fold the book to store it.

Children can make an accordion book to keep a record of books they have read. Make several copies of the train cars to use.

# My Writing Log

Name _____

| My ideas for writing: | I wrote my first copy. | I made changes. | I published my writing. |
|---|---|---|---|
| | | | |
| | | | |
| | | | |
| | | | |
| | | | |

Make copies of the Writing Log for children to keep in their portfolios. Keep a log of progress by placing check marks, a rubber stamp, or a date for each writing idea that is developed.

Rigby Best Teachers Press
101 Ways... SV 141901885X